PAPUA NEW GUINEA

Tales from a Wild Island

PAPUA NEW GUINEA

Tales from a Wild Island

Howard M. Beck

Robert Hale · London

© *Howard M. Beck 2009*
First published in Great Britain 2009

ISBN 978 0 7090 8449 5

Robert Hale Limited
Clerkenwell House
Clerkenwell Green
London EC1R 0HT

www.halebooks.com

A catalogue record for this book is available from the British Library

2 4 6 8 10 9 7 5 3 1

Printed in China
and arranged by New Era Printing Co Ltd, Hong Kong

Contents

Acknowledgements

I would like to thank everyone who played a part in the genesis of this book, not least my New Guinea friends, the native porters and guides, and all who have played a role in the following narrative. I must also thank Dave Brook for permission to reproduce images from the British caving expedition. Last, but certainly not least, my appreciation goes to my publisher John Hale and of his staff for their input, patience and professionalism.

Notes on the Photography

Unless otherwise acknowledged, all of the photographs in this book are the work of the author. Equipment used was a Nikon 35mm SLR fitted with standard, 35mm and 108mm lenses.

List of Illustrations

Introduction

Described as still using Stone Age technology, the Liawep were almost naked and appeared to have had no contact with the outside world. They spoke a language unlike any others in the vicinity and displayed astonishment at the sight of steel tools, such as axes and machetes. A cameo from the turn of the twentieth century? *Au contraire*. These nomads, living in the wild territory between Telefomin and Oksapmin, at the very centre of Papua New Guinea, were only discovered in the late 1990s when a routine government patrol made first contact.

The wild hinterland of Papua New Guinea has vast swathes of mountainous terrain, rugged in the extreme and clothed in virgin rain forest. By virtue of this geographical isolation new tribes like the Liawep are still occasionally encountered. Numbering only seventy-nine individuals, this secretive tribe are just one of the many anachronisms that go into making this such a wonderfully unique and unpredictable country.

Wild, untamed, rugged, unpredictable – these were just the adjectives to fire my imagination. It has been said that an optimist is a person who sees opportunity in a difficulty, and a pessimist is one who sees difficulty in an opportunity. I like to think of myself as the former, and although all our lives are governed by chance and fate, travel is still about seizing opportunities, making spontaneous decisions, surprises, disappointments and last-minute changes of plans.

My interest in New Guinea was assured many years ago with the reading of such classic accounts as *Across New Guinea from the Fly to the Sepik*, *Patrol into Yesterday* and *The Land That Time Forgot*. When an opportunity to travel presented itself, I excitedly recalled such accounts. Papua New Guinea would, I was sure, present all manner of unforeseen obstacles and confrontations; I hoped I might cope with these, and rise to the challenges that ultimately would enrich my overall experience.

Some time ago I unearthed my long-lost diaries and notes, and began poring over them, reliving the dramatic sequence of events that had swept me along during my time in-country. As I turned the pages it became clear to me that I must record the details of these encounters and marshal them in a format that others could enjoy. This book is the result.

The events and the characters are factual, supported by diaries and the notes I made at the time, additionally layered through with slabs of background information reinforcing each stratum of my adventures. The latter were fraught and uplifting in equal measure, and span a four-year period, including an eight-month sentence in the trackless jungles lying at the heart of the country. So join me now on a wild journey of discovery in a land that is quite literally 'like every place you've never been'.

1 Don't Get Etten bi the Cannibals

Cruising at a height of 39,000 feet and 500 mph there is no turning back. I picked over my lunch with all the enthusiasm of a condemned man, at the same time gazing out of the scratched window of the aircraft. This afforded me a Claude Glass view of the roiling clouds below. Ruminating on the fact that I was bound for a land infamous for its cannibal and headhunting propensities, I wondered if there were any lingering tendencies, still, for its blood-thirsty past.

Having done a little research I knew that Papua New Guinea extended almost to 179,000 square miles in extent and was the last inhabited place on earth to be 'discovered' by Old World explorers. Further, I learned that this unbelievably rugged country is populated by around 5½ million people, Melanesians, divided into 10,000 tribal groups, speaking an amazing 800 distinct languages.

There are at least 100 species of snake, 3,000 orchids, spiders the size of saucers and tribal fights as regular as European football fixtures. The local form of justice is known as 'pay-back', and the biggest taboo is, on pain of death, to run over and kill a pig. With all these facts to mull over during the mind-numbing flight, my destiny, I suspected, was about to take a colourful twist.

The island of New Guinea, though geographically slipped between the timeless land mass of Australia and the equator, is even today a relatively mysterious land. At the cross-roads of South-east Asia, it lies severed from the Far East, where the Indonesian archipelago melts away into the sun-kissed south-west Pacific.

In outline, it is not unlike a reposing beast, facing west with jaws agape, seemingly about to devour the Moluccas islands of Ceram and Misool. PNG, as Papua New Guinea is known, is the eastern half of the island, as opposed to Irian Jaya, the Indonesian western half. It is as isolated as one can imagine, romantic but remote, beautiful yet savage, and very often referred to still as the 'Last Unknown'.

I have always loved geography, and at primary school my imagination was kindled by places whose names rang almost with mythical quality – Lapland, Patagonia, Tibet – but the siren call of the great unknown without doubt was the singular island of New Guinea. Half a lifetime would pass before I could answer that call.

As luck would have it, a friend of a friend knew someone else acquainted with an Australian in PNG. He was desperate to recruit a European motor vehicle engineer. In the blink of an eye, it seemed, I had an employment contract for at least two years and a golden opportunity for some first-hand adventure and exploration. In short order I was packed and on my way to the Western Highlands of this wildest of untamed lands.

In Sydney I discovered that there was no connecting flight to Port Moresby for three whole days. So the next day I visited Papua New Guinea House to confirm that my immigration documents were in order. I was greeted with a blithe 'g'day' by an officious-looking sort, with skin redolent of days idled away on sun-drenched beaches, seated behind an oversized desk presided over by the union jack and six stars of the Australian flag.[1] With a cursory glance at my documents his cheerful demeanour dissolved into a frown and he announced that my visa was invalid.

There were no 'buts'. I would, he offered with an expression of bored insouciance, be returned to Australia on the first available plane. Panic set in, as by this time I had only a few dollars to my name. I could not afford any further delay.

My protestations that the document had been issued by his counterparts back in London fell on deaf ears. However, another sun-bronzed official appeared, and to my utter relief pointed out that in fact my permit was just fine. Two days later I made my way to the airport clutching my precious visa, and with my last few cents jangling in my pocket, I was on my way north at last.

Now we began flying a wide circle, at the same time rapidly losing height over low savannah-covered hills threaded by dusty tracks which linked groups of tin-roofed dwellings glistening in the sun like a scattered herd of shiny armadillos. Dotted about this sprawling excuse for suburbia were parched gardens that would hardly have looked out of place in the Middle East. Here and there turquoise rectangles betrayed the dwellings of the well-to-do – mostly expats, I guessed.

I was taken aback by the arid-looking landscape. The red earth was anomalous in this, one of the wettest places on earth. A follically challenged, middle-aged gentleman was seated next to me. He had been buried in a book all the way from Brisbane, but seeing me staring out the window, he suddenly became animated.

'New here?'

'Yes, first time in the tropics.' Is it that obvious? I thought.

'Welcome to PNG,' he said with a smile.

'Dry, isn't it?' I observed, probably showing surprise.

'It's the rain shadow,' he said with authority. 'Port Moresby is sheltered from the north-west monsoons by the proximity of the Owen Stanleys[2] away north.' He set down his book.

These cloud-grazing mountains, he went on to explain, formed the eastern extremity of the 1,500 mile long central cordillera of mainland New Guinea, a major range of mountains extending from Milne Bay westwards to the Vogelkop (bird's head) Peninsula in Irian Jaya. The mountains represented the loftiest ground between the Himalayas and the Andes.[3] I asked about rainfall.

'This time of year? Hardly any. Moresby usually gets about forty inches a year.'

Parts of England receive that much, I thought. 'Doesn't sound much for the tropics,' I said.

'No, six hundred's what you call rain. Western Province. Don't ever go there, my friend, it's hundreds of square miles of nothing. Just endless swamp, mosquitoes and bush. Damned rain never stops.'

How much time have you spent in the jungle then?

The Owen Stanley range, he informed me, was famous for the Kokoda Trail. Linking the north and south coasts, this jungle path was first used by miners heading for the Kokoda gold fields of the 1890s. Later, during the Second World War, Australians fought a fierce battle along this jungle corridor to repel invading Japanese who, in their 'back door' attempt to capture the capital, had slogged across the mountains from the north-east. In September 1942, at a place called Ioribaiwa Ridge, the enemy advance had been turned back literally within sight of Moresby.

With jungle warfare just a vague memory for a dwindling handful of surviving veterans, travel in the equatorial forest today means different things to different people. The Kokoda Trail is now a gruelling back-packers' route. It is challenging, even without being shot at, involving a total ascent of at least 18,000 feet over 60 miles. It reaches a high point on Mount Bellamy at 6,900 feet, where with luck and clear air, a rare enough occurrence in the steamy tropics, it is just possible to see both coasts.

Once in the 'bush', as Australians affectionately call the forest, one soon develops a strange affinity with nature. This is an inescapable facet of jungle travel, like the mud and the mosquitoes – to some it is utopia, and others simply hell on earth. I could not even begin to imagine what it must have been like in those jungle-choked heights, as a young soldier, coping and trying to stay alive.

My impromptu history lesson was interrupted by the squeal of rubber as we touched down at Moresby airport. The pilot taxied the plane across the apron toward a single-storey terminal building. Here I noticed people dressed in colourful attire massed beyond a chain link fence. They reminded me of a flock of gaudy parakeets. I rescued my carry-on bag from the overhead locker and joined those waiting to disembark. The outside had looked hot from within the cabin, but when I stepped through the door and went down the steps to the shim-mering concrete, I thought, someone's left the oven door open. God only knew why I was wearing corduroy trousers and my best Harris tweed jacket, but as Noel Coward once said, 'Mad dogs and Englishmen …'

The humidity wrapped itself around me like a wet blanket, remind-ing me that I was only a few degrees shy of the equator. After barely two dozen steps, rivulets of perspiration sprang from between my shoulder blades. It was then I noticed that hallmark of tropical airports everywhere, the cloying smell of avgas, rubber and deep-scented flow-ering shrubs.

The air was barely less humid inside the arrivals hall. Hall was perhaps a little too ostentatious a word. A couple of geriatric ceiling fans transplanted from a Humphrey Bogart movie were struggling to stir the heavy air. They were wobbling so badly that I gave them a wide berth, convinced that they would crash to the floor any moment, bring-ing with them the cracked and peeling plasterwork.

Welcome to Jackson's Airport, Papua New Guinea, the tropics.

Unlike larger international airports, there was none of the sophistication, or modern baggage handling facilities one might expect. Joining the cosmopolitan jamboree in the frenetic hunt for my suitcase, I wondered where on earth to begin. My shirt and trousers were by this time clinging like a second skin. All of the luggage had been off-loaded into one large chaotic heap among which other foreigners and PNG nationals alike were delving for their precious belongings. Children were running around, screaming and laughing, everyone talking at once. An infant crying.

The pile contained a mixture of suitcases, sacks and shapeless string bags. There were pushchairs, and Japanese-made ghetto blasters, and parasols. Even a birdcage. I saw a guitar that was the worse for wear, threadbare rucksacks and unmentionables that challenged close scrutiny. It reminded me of a badly organized rummage sale.

I would have laughed but for the fact the humidity was sapping my energy as surely as if I had contracted some insidious tropical malaise. I spotted the 'oracle' drawing a wheeled suitcase in a wake of perspiration. Our eyes briefly met and we exchanged perfunctory waves.

I returned to the task in hand.

Occasionally I glanced at my watch. The check-in time for my connecting flight to the Highlands gradually came – and passed. I felt anxiety building to a blood-vessel-bursting crescendo. I peeled off my jacket like a python shedding last season's skin, but this made precious little difference to my discomfort. Worse, my green suitcase remained elusive.

It was only when the unruly drift of human jetsam had dwindled to just one battered holdall and an empty crisp packet that I realized, belatedly, that my expensive new case was probably still in Sydney, Heathrow even. I set about reporting the loss, a task not made easier by the woman filling out the forms. She asked the most inane questions.

'Where did you last see your luggage?'

'In London,' I said.

'How do you know it's lost?' she asked in a teacher-knows-best tone.

'Because it's not here in Port Moresby,' I replied with impeccable logic.

'What colour is your suitcase?'

'Green.'

'Is there anything to distinguish it?'

'Yes, it's green,' I almost barked.

I almost lost it at this point. The humidity was sapping my patience and I was ready to snap. All she had to do to push me over the brink was ask me my date of birth or the colour of my father's eyes, or something equally irrelevant. She was testing me, I decided, and took three deep breaths to calm my jangling nerves.

'How big is it?'

'Big enough not to go missing.' And so it went on for several more minutes. I eventually completed the process without being arrested for murder and made my way to the next stage of the game, expecting I would never see my luggage again in this lifetime.

Up the Purari Without a Paddle

As a British subject holding a valid visa my entry into PNG was a mere formality. Without any bags it was made even easier. I was through immigration in the blink of an eye. My connecting flight to the Highlands had been delayed, but by this time the Air Niugini Fokker was spooling up and taxiing slowly away from the terminal. As I watched the shimmering image of the plane recede I saw with it my chances of reaching the interior, my destination that day.

'*Yu laik kisim balus i go?*'

'Eh?' I turned to see someone I took to be a cleaner from the way he was dressed, though equally he might have been an airline official.

'Yes, me want go long Hagen,' I responded in hastily contrived Pidgin English.

'*Dispela balus em i go nau.*' With a vague gesture he motioned for me to catch up with the plane by running and leaping inside. It took me just a few seconds to realize he was serious, and a few more to notice the cabin door had yet to be closed. Feeling a little like the arch-villain in a Bond movie, and notwithstanding my attire, I sprinted across the apron in hot pursuit. To my utter astonishment the plane came to a momentary standstill, I was roughly grasped, then hoisted aboard in a quite undignified manner.

'*Pasin bilong Niugini* (the way of things in New Guinea),' an air hostess said, slamming the door shut and sealing it behind me.

'Right,' I managed to gasp before flopping into the nearest vacant window seat and buckling myself in for the one and a half hour flight. '*Pasin bilong Niugini*' was an expression I was to encounter many times over the coming months, used to explain away all manner of delays, problems and frustrations.

To reach Mount Hagen, some 5,500 feet above sea level, we proceeded north-west along the mangrove-serried coastline of the Gulf of Papua as far as the Purari delta at Orokolo Bay. New Guinea has the kind of interactive weather for which Britain is renowned, only more of it, considerably more. The mighty Purari is one of four principal rivers carrying this annual deluge from the mountainous hinterland down to the sea. From its outfall into the Gulf the river's winding course is used by pilots as a signpost into the Highlands, and ultimately to the populated valley systems[4] that until the 1930s no one even suspected existed.

Owing to the nature of the terrain and the capricious weather, all internal flights use line of sight, navigation done by dead reckoning aided by familiar landmarks such as rivers and prominent peaks, and aviation charts. Since clouds build up quickly throughout the mountains, all domestic flights consequently take place as early in the day as possible.

Soon we were banking to the north and heading for the interior. The view became one expanse of primary forest resembling a vast table of badly laid green baize. Peering down at the trees I saw sunlight shimmering off the coffee-coloured, serpentine waters of the Purari, sometimes reflected in a placid lagoon, or a secretive loop of a jungle creek momentarily revealed by breaks in the forest canopy.

I had a bird's-eye glimpse of a remote little clearing containing two bush huts from which wisps of blue smoke drifted lazily into the air. I could practically smell the wood fires and wondered who lived there, and what they might be thinking as our plane droned overhead like a blowfly on the windowpane of their isolated world.

We flew on for another half hour, by which time the sight of endless trees was beginning to pall. Soon the high mountains started to appear. We slipped between the Aure and Keieru ranges on a north-west heading. The next major landmarks were the isolated Mount Karimui to the starboard, and the MacGregor peaks on our left, after which, some 170 miles from the coast, the Purari divided into the Erave, joining from the west, and the Tua. Following the latter we headed east-north-east, circumventing the striated northern flanks of Karimui.

Very soon we were flying through a jumble of rugged mountains and interlocking spurs, their harsh geology softened by the comprehensive forest mantle, only the highest summits occasionally thrusting their bare bones into the tropical air. Those unfamiliar with the route into the Highlands, including myself, cast anxious eyes through the windows as lonely summits loomed out of the clouds either side, then vanished again just as quickly as they had appeared. There seemed no way around, let alone through the mountains. The atmosphere aboard the plane became distinctly palpable.

Flight has always been fraught in this part of the world. But, it has played an important role throughout the history of the country, in modern times proving equally vital for its transport infrastructure. Despite its hazardous nature, today more journeys are undertaken by air than by road, and there are more airstrips per capita than in almost any other country.

The main Highlands Highway, along which most everyday necessities are transported, is mostly a rough, unsurfaced road, hazardous in the extreme. It extends from the east-coast port of Lae through the Eastern Highlands, the Simbu and Western Highlands, to the Porgera gold mine in the Enga Province, and to Mendi in the Southern Highlands.

Additionally there are hundreds of miles of minor, arterial bush tracks fit only for 4x4s, snaking off to places with names that excite curiosity: Lake Kutubu, Nambaiyufa, Tabibuga and Lufa. Other road networks focus upon provincial centres such as Madang and Wewak, though surprisingly PNG is one of the few countries where the capital has no road links with other major population centres.

We banked a little to starboard. Knife-edged arêtes drifted by just a little too close for comfort as isolated forest giants, poking their ragged crowns out of the swirling mists, seemed intent on plucking our frail craft from the sky. There was a collective sigh from the thirty or so passengers when the threatening peaks suddenly parted and a vast grassy plain spread before us like a welcome mat.

The broad green valley stretched away into the distance, perhaps 10 miles wide, and ten times that in length, flanked by mountains, the summits of which I had read were just a tad short of 3 miles high. A broad river, the Wahgi, could be seen meandering through grasslands that appeared from altitude like a manicured bowling green, but as I would later discover, in reality consisted of stifling sword grasses growing as much as 6 feet tall.

Here and there the broad valley floor swelled into low grassy hills

View down the Baiyer Valley from the gorge road leading from Mount Hagen

and roller-coaster ridges. Clusters of oblong thatched huts dotted the valley floor, and everywhere, including much of the lower mountain slopes, was a chequerboard of neatly arranged garden plots. Rising smoke here and there betrayed the continuing slash and burn agrarian policy that is still a feature of everyday Highlands life.

Having done my homework, I knew that the first white men into these valleys were prospectors hoping to find gold in the creeks and rivers. Some found their fortune, others an early grave, yet all were astonished to discover that, contrary to popular belief, the interior consisted of a series of valleys heavily populated by tall warrior farmers. The peoples of the Wahgi, for instance, cultivated *kau-kau* (sweet potato), and had a penchant for wearing Napoleonesque wigs fashioned from human hair. They had pig tusks through their nasal septums and carried fine blackpalm spears; tribal conflict was as much a daily part of their lives as is a visit from the postman in Western countries.

Touch-down at Hagen's airport was uneventful, but the contrast with Moresby could not have been more marked. Here there was none of the sticky atmosphere of the coast. As I left the plane the clouds, I noticed, were already flirting with the highest mountains enclosing the valley. The Highlands benefit from a pleasant spring-like climate all year round, which I was to discover was hot – like an exceptional English high summer day – by day and pleasantly cool after dusk. Gone too were the worst of the tropical scourges, as well as the mosquitoes which, though still present, were not in numbers sufficient to become traumatic.

An airline official told me that Hagen township was a ten-minute drive down the only metalled road, but that quite fortuitously my new boss lived just a short walk away, here in Kagamuga. Everyone evidently knew Brian Heagney, for as well as the Autoport, where I would be working, he was also owner of coffee plantations, and a haulage company plying the Highlands Highway. I casually strolled out of the airport, to be greeted by a sun borrowed from a spaghetti western.

All the houses, I noticed, had gardens trimmed with colourful hibiscus, poinsettia and other exotic flowering shrubs peculiar to these latitudes. The single-floor Heagney residence was balanced on 3 foot timber piles and of a lightweight construction I recognized as post-war fibreboard. The ubiquitous corrugated tin roof completed the design, also providing run-off for rainwater. This was collected in a storage tank and subsequently pumped up into a header vessel. I noted some banana plantains growing beside the water tank, their leaves ragged and turning brown along the edges.

Strutting onto the verandah, I rapped with a knuckle on the fly screen door. The inner door proper was agape, allowing me a glimpse into a room that seemed cavern-like compared with the bright sunlight out of doors. I could hear a hound yapping somewhere close by, and a line of ants, I saw, was walking single-file up the door frame, strung out on some urgent errand of survival.

With a look of puzzlement a ferret of a man with skin like brown parchment came to the door.

'Brian Heagney?' I ventured.

'Yeah,' he said. 'Wad ya want?'

'Your new mechanic,' I replied extending a hand. There were further looks of bewilderment. 'From England. Howard Beck.'

'Oh. Yeah, the Pommie mechanic. Right, well, yeah, *yeah*. Wad the hell you doing here? Wasn't expecting you for a couple more weeks at least.'

I gave a nervous sort of laugh, recalling the initial difficulties I had experienced in Sydney. 'Well,' I replied. 'Here I am. Pleased to meet you.'

'Come on in,' he said, indicating an old cane chair by a louvre window.

With a sigh I parked my weary frame. Heagney made for the cooler. 'Beer?' Not waiting for an answer he dropped a chilled can of Tooheys in my lap. 'Where's your luggage?' he asked.

'Lost, most likely still in Sydney,' I said.

'Ah well,' he replied, sitting down. He told me I might get lucky, but his tone left hope wanting. I gained the impression that he was used to property disappearing and things never happening. He had the appearance of a man who had grown out of the land, or at least survived here long enough to have taken root. 'Gone troppo' I later learned was the term in common parlance. We cracked a couple more 'tinnies' and then he offered to run me into town to show me my accommodation and place of work.

Frontier Town

Hagen's sole metalled road, part of the main Highlands Highway, extended between the airport and the town, beyond both of which it degenerated into a dirt course full of physical challenges. On the way into town I noticed that the road was mostly flanked by dense forest, separated from the road by drainage ditches (*barats*) to carry away the heavy downpours of the wet season. These trenches appeared so deep I was convinced that a vehicle leaving the road would disappear for good. I made a mental note to remember this.

The weather pattern in this part of the south-west Pacific is governed by two wind systems, the north-west monsoon between December and April, and the south-east trades from May to October. This, however, is an over-simplification of a picture that is further complicated by micro-climates created by the island's rugged interior. In this part of the country, Heagney told me, the wet season occurred between October and April when 80 inches of rain was usual, though the tendency was

A Mount Hagen village *sing-sing*. All the men are wearing Napoleonic-style wigs of human hair and woven aprons. Some are beating kundu drums, others are waving black palm spears

for it to rain even in the dry season, creating the impression of wet and wetter seasons rather than a distinct wet-dry division.

Breaks in the forest gave way to graceful stands of bamboo and casuarina, or offered a glimpse of areas planted with coffee laid out in neat rows, their dark, glossy leaves contrasting with the bright scarlet of the ripening beans. Piles of freshly hewn firewood stacked on the verge awaited potential buyers. I stuck my head out of the passenger window to take in the alien bouquet of my new home: the smell reminded me of a botanical garden with just a hint of wood smoke.

Battered Toyota Landcruisers were going this way and that, I noticed, as well as the occasional truck, mostly bursting with people of all ages. The roadsides were throng with folk milling about. Women, their necks swathed in masses of tiny, colourful beads, were mincing along with bunches of bananas on their heads or boxes of Black Swan or San Miguel lager stacked two high. Trailing in their wake were snotty-nosed children, bare-footed, some wielding huge, shiny machetes. One young boy was leading a sorry-looking pig by a string tied to one of its front ankles.

Men seemed to be strutting along doing nothing in particular, some brandishing bow and arrows, others decked out in traditional finery, all of them carrying straight-shafted axes tucked into a belt. I spied one fellow proudly sporting a black umbrella with more holes than material.

Groups of people were gathered around cases of booze stacked by the wayside. Heagney noted my interest. 'Pay day,' he said with a nod in their direction. 'For those that have jobs. They blow it all on beer, make a nuisance of themselves, then sober up and wait for next pay day.' He grunted.

Without exception all the women had a bulging string carry-all, known as a *billum*, suspended down their back from a carrying strap slipped around the forehead. The gathered people were apparently awaiting a PMV (Public Motor Vehicle), a Toyota pick-up and the nearest thing to a taxi in PNG.

Dress for both sexes appeared to be a woven apron suspended from a sort of cane or, in some cases, tree bark, cuirass, with a bustle of cordyline leaves known as 'arse grass' to the Europeans, tucked into the back as a concession to modesty. Those adopting Western dress seemed to favour shorts, with or without a tee-shirt, and for the women unbecoming printed cotton shifts resembling maternity smocks. Some women opted for the bare-breasted look. Clothing, for the most part, was filthy and full of holes, the tee-shirts bearing totally incongruous slogans such as 'Support the Iditarod Dog Sled Race', though more commonly they proclaimed the virtues of the local brew.

We entered town. Shunning ceremony Heagney showed me my workplace, handed over the key to an adjacent flat and left me to it. I was eager to go out to see the town, and with my luggage anywhere between PNG and London, I desperately needed some tropical clothing to be going on with. I received an advance on my salary, dropped my few belongings on the creaky bed and was soon heading up Moka Place towards the town centre.

I passed a PMV stop (more crowds and cases of beer) and the offices of the Department of Lands and Surveys, turned left into Romba Street, and left again into a wide, dusty thoroughfare labelled Hagen Drive, and that was it. Drive through too fast and risk missing it.

Main street of Hagen township

The main street was divided by a central island that was an optimistic reservation for balding grass, straggly hibiscus bushes and tall, alien-looking spiky bromeliads. On either side angle-parking was the norm, ranks of Holden sedans, pick-ups of Japanese manufacture and the odd Mini Moke being representative of the vehicles present, all disguised beneath a copious veneer of dust and mud. Everything about the town had a tired look.

There was the usual collection of stores one might expect in any western town, but mostly of prefabricated or clapboard construction with about as much charm as an industrial estate. They resembled fortresses, protected with bars and chain-linked shutters. I enquired of a passer-by what this was all about, and was told it was a defence against the nightly attention of 'rascals'. Each evening, apparently, the shutters were lowered portcullis-like over doors and windows.

'Rascals' (*raskol* in Pidgin) are a uniquely PNG phenomenon. No schoolboy pranksters here, rather local 'hoods' who think little of breaking into stores or houses, and carrying off whatever takes their fancy. *Pasin bilong Niugini.*

Apart from several Chinese trade stores, there was a pharmacy, a newsagent, a couple of hotels, a post office, and electrical supplies outlet, clothing shops and three supermarket-type stores: New Guinea

Company, Burns Philp and Steamships Trading. Located on the outskirts of town was the hospital (*haus sic* in Pidgin), and a corrugated tin cinema (*haus picsa*), also known engagingly as the house flea.

It was hard to believe that at the turn of the last century Hagen did not exist. At that time the pace of exploration in the Highlands was governed by gold. There had been major strikes further east, near Bulolo in Morobe Province, and so rich were these that in the 1930s $30 million of the precious metal had been exported and the search for new fields renewed.

Many characters were struck by gold fever – the likes of 'Shark-eye' Park, Charlie Gough, 'Tiger Lil' and a dog named Towzer that licked up several ounces of gold dust from a pan. The owner tied the dog to a sluice, dosed it with castor oil then waited while his gold reappeared! Gold even attracted a handsome young Australian called Errol Flynn, prior to his swashbuckling Hollywood days. For a while he worked his own mine some few miles outside Port Moresby, but seemingly left the country under suspicious circumstances, owing money.

During a patrol in 1930 two seasoned prospectors, Mick Dwyer and Mick Leahy, crossed the island from the headwaters of the Ramu southwards into the catchment of the Purari. During their three-month expedition a new and much larger river was found joining the Purari from the west. Over several days a number of bloated corpses were seen floating down the river which, they believed, were indicative of a large and unknown population further to the west. The new river turned out to be the Wahgi.

In a series of prospecting patrols, jointly financed by the New Guinea Goldfields Company and the Government, an advance base and airstrip was established first at Bena Bena in the Asaro Valley, in what today is the Eastern Highlands, and from there an aerial reconnaissance, soon followed by a foot patrol, eventually entered the large and populous Wahgi Valley.

On 27 April 1933 a single-engined de Havilland Fox Moth lifted off from Bena Bena piloted by Ian Grabowsky. A short while later and further west, he landed in the new valley, at a rudimentary earthen airstrip hastily prepared by Mike Leahy and patrol officer Jim Taylor at a place called Wilya, at the south-western end of where Hagen is today. Standing over 6 feet tall, Grabowsky climbed down from the belly of the giant 'bird' wearing white coveralls and large green goggles. The locals had never seen anything like this, and without exception the tall,

bellicose warriors prostrated themselves on the ground and wailed. So
Hagen town came into being.

Since those heady prospecting
days it has grown into a bustling
centre with a population of around
8,000, a cultural melting pot of
European expatriates – German and
Dutch, British and Australians of
course, a few Americans – as well as
indigenous New Guineans, together
with a leavening of Chinese and
Filippinos. It appeared that the
Australians did as little as possible,
while the Chinese mostly ran the
trade stores, which sold everything
from food supplies to cooking pots,
guitars, clothing and bedding.

PMVs were almost continually
disgorging or sweeping up rag-tag
packs of villagers plying the trade
stores, or coming into town either to
hawk their wares or simply to loiter
or socialize in the streets with
wantoks.[5] The men were tall, proud
and bearded, and strutted up and
down with confident bearing and
strong features resembling ancient
Assyrians.

A young Hagen woman
wearing her second-best
head-dress for a *sing-sing*

Tropical issue for the expatriates
or sophisticated nationals appeared mostly to be shorts and, in the case
of Australians, white knee-length socks, while European women
favoured slacks or lightweight cotton frocks. I noticed a local woman,
her face painted in striking tribal colours, working at a checkout in one
of the larger stores, while some old men (*lapun*) dressed in *lap-lap* and
'arse grass' mooched about the pavements and roadside verges. The
older men often carried handbags, not as a fashion statement, merely a
practical solution to the age old problem of where to carry one's *buai*[6]
and how to keep cigarettes dry when 'arse grass' and *lap-lap* have a

conspicuous lack of pockets. I found it endearing the way they would hold these bags draped over one arm.

I found Robert Cheung's, a large trading emporium where I was able to buy clothing I required, as well as a suitable sun hat and some strong footwear more in keeping with my new surroundings.

The whole place had a distinct 'wild west' feel to it, enhanced by the dust and grime, the ramshackle vehicles, and the noisy but colourful throng of people going about their livelihood. The pioneering atmosphere was further emphasized by the tangled jungle which was constantly searching and prying at the town's threshold. The forest seemed somehow expectant, as if biding its time until the day it could send in its legions of tendrils, tenacious vines and strangling lianas, to win back what had temporarily been relinquished to Western amenity. It brought to mind a few words of Rudyard Kipling:

> I will let loose against you the fleet-footed vines –
> I will call in the jungle to stamp out your lines.[7]

Don't Get Hung by the Kanakas

My missing suitcase turned up the week after my arrival, appearing mysteriously on my doorstep with no explanation. That none of my belongings was missing was even more miraculous.

One weekend almost a month after my arrival, enjoying a welcome break from diesel engines and trucks, I was in town watching a gaggle of tribesmen on the pavement arguing over a pathetic handful of tobacco leaves, when I realized something that had been puzzling me since my arrival. The people appeared to be at a halfway house in life, neither here nor there; not quite fully integrated into Western ways, and clearly in a sort of sartorial state of limbo. Many of the men, for instance, were dressed neither wholly traditionally nor *pasin bilong masta* (in the Western style). One would wear 'arse grass' along with a tee-shirt, another a pair of shorts complemented by the most extravagant birds' plumage head-dress. I noted that whatever the chosen dress, some tribesmen would be painted, a pig tusk piercing the nose, others not. I thought in a way it was all rather sad, for these people had clearly not been absorbed into, or benefited from, the ways of the West, yet had been sufficiently tainted by it for some no longer to fit comfortably in either camp.

Young Hagen man wearing a
spectacular head-dress of
eagle feathers and Raggiena
bird of paradise

Thoroughly absorbed in my people watching I blundered straight into a tall fellow carrying a vicious-looking blackpalm spear. He had on a bird-wing 'helmet' fashioned, I think, from vivid red parrot feathers, which gave to him the appearance of Hermes the Greek god of thieves and commerce. 'Sorry,' I blurted out without thinking, then with a more measured response, guessing that he might be one of the local 'rascals', or possibly even Chief Accountant for Steamship Trading, '*Gude moning wantok* (good morning friend).'

'Moning, *masta*', he grinned through a mouthful of blackened teeth, before dredging up a huge gob of red buai juice and spitting it all over a nearby litter bin. With a passing whiff of rancid pig grease he moved on, vacantly gazing into store windows. I noted that the bin was overflowing with corn husks and sugar cane chewings, and blood-red blotches of betel nut decorated the bin and the ground all about.

Back at the flat Manga, my *haus boi*, handed me a pot of tea. 'Don't get etten bi the cannibals' were the tongue-in-cheek parting words of a fellow Yorkshireman back in England. They were still ringing in my ears after my first month in this raw land, when Manga pulled me aside for some useful advice.

'*Masta. Yu mas nogat kilim kanaka, pikinini or pik long kar bilong yu.*'

'Oh,' I replied, not knowing what the hell a *kanaka* was.

'*Kanaka, em i dai pinis, yu bai dai. Em tasol,*' he continued with a smirk and a tone that to me suggested amusement at my mystified expression.

It was nothing really, I soon discovered. If I drove over anyone, or their pig, and death resulted, then their kinsmen would kill me. It was nothing personal, just the pay-back system in operation. Simple. An eye for an eye, the most ruthless form of bush justice.

A *kanaka*, it turned out, was the somewhat derogatory term Europeans used for a PNG aboriginal. 'Don't get hung by the *kanakas*' was a jocular warning often given by seasoned expatriates to anyone new going into the bush for the very first time.

I considered the lesson. If one was involved in an accident resulting in the death of a villager, the safest course of action was to hightail it out of the country. The threat of reprisals was so acute that, as I understood it, a condition of entry into the country was to lodge a bond equivalent to a one-way air fare out. I had not been party to this and assumed my bond had been arranged by my employer.

The best advice was to go immediately to the police station for protective custody, though because of the *wantok* system even this does not necessarily guarantee safety. Better still, get out of the country altogether. Yes, I thought as I sipped my cup of finest locally grown Kurumul leaf, there was no doubt my new life was going to be a wholly different experience.

Apart from the airport, the Highlands Highway (*Bikpela Rot Bilong Ol*), potentially fraught as it might be, was the town's lifeline, along which most necessities of survival, other than those that could be flown in, were freighted from the east coast. The road passed through town and continued west to Togoba. It represented my 'open sesame' to untold adventure; I could barely contain my eagerness to be off exploring.

The forest to the English would always be 'jungle', whereas Australians preferred the term 'bush', which could refer to any territory beyond civilization, which I suppose included most of the country. As a consequence the Pidgin for jungle was *Bikpela Bus*. I heard that in the *Bikpela Bus* not far out of town were some large and impressive caves. Their existence gave rise to an early opportunity for exploration and a chance to practise my Pidgin (*Tok Pisin*).

The Kum Caves were secreted in the foothills of a mountain range to the south, and accessed initially by 4x4 along an ascending bush track about an hour out of town. It was late afternoon and, having left the Toyota behind, I tramped with a guide across the Kuta Ridge and waded for about thirty minutes down a shallow creek, hoping nothing with fangs lurked in the murky water. Leaving the stream we climbed the bank and pushed our way through tall pit-pit grass, wet patches of perspiration staining my shirt. And still there was no hint of the promised caves.

We had just passed through a patch of regrowth when I at last spied what looked suspiciously like a void partway up a steep, forested buttress. Wisps of mist were raking the eminence, looking like a romantic Chinese landscape painting. I was about to investigate when, as if from nowhere, the undergrowth parted and a wizened old crone stepped into view. It transpired that she was the wife of the landowner, or *papa bilong graun*.

There is no twilight so close to the equator and darkness falls with a suddenness unknown in more temperate climes. With the shadows of early evening lengthening and the cave (*hul bilong ston*) beckoning, I was

Not everything in the undergrowth is friendly as in the case of this spiny lawyer cane

anxious to explore it and return to town before nightfall. Impatiently, I indicated the entrance, pointing at the flying fox streaming from it like black rags before a gale-blast.

'*Wanem nem bilong em*? (What are they called?)' I asked.

'*Blak bokis*,' replied the old woman.

'*Blak bokis bilong meri*?' I ventured, in my attempt to establish if her family owned the creatures as well as the cave. Her expression instantly changed.

My guide pulled me to one side for a discreet lesson in Pidgin. It transpired that, while *blak bokis* is indeed the name for flying fox, it is also a term with dual connotation, and in my haste I had unwittingly made some embarrassing reference to the intimate nether regions of the old woman.

'Er, no ... No! *Nogat tru*. Cave. Hole *bilong* stone. Flying foxes *tasol*,' I said in a fluster of English and hopeless Pidgin, flapping my arms in a further red-faced and quite fruitless attempt at explanation. 'Bats!' I said finally. I was only making matters worse. With a rustle of undergrowth, and muttering something I suspect was not complimentary, the woman vanished as suddenly as she had appeared.

In the event the cave was of little interest, merely a single tunnel floored with mud deposits and countless years' accumulation of bat droppings. Many of the creatures were still suspended from the roof, hanging there screeching, the acrid smell of ammonia making us gag as our boots crunched about a floor seething with many-legged creeping and slithery things.

The large but short section of fossil passage plunged straight through a small limestone spur and was, at best, only a few hundred feet in length. However, the view from the entrance, of misty forested mountains spilling down around us, was some compensation for my disappointment. I returned to Hagen hopeful of better things to come.

2 Laughing Death

Having been in the country about six weeks I was still trying to overcome my initial shock upon seeing the Hagen Autoport. Back in England the name had conjured up pictures of a modern, well-equipped vehicle repair facility, but it was in reality simply a dump – and I am probably being generous at that. Crestfallen, I settled into a round of truck repairs and sleep – Monday to Friday soon becoming simply the days leading to Saturday and Sunday. I longed for some genuine adventure.

While up to my neck in widgets and oily things my mind would frequently wing off at a tangent, my waking dreams filling with images of bottomless caves, mist-shrouded mountain heights, large and wondrous insects, pythons and birds of paradise. Equally, my night-mares were haunted by a boundless jungle wilderness peopled by primitive tribes killing and eating one another.

One morning I awoke with the bed gyrating. *Earthquake*, I thought as I sprang out of bed. It was my third since arriving in the country – nothing unusual there. Swaying across the living room, my eyes focused just in time to witness the previous night's beer glasses enacting a two-step towards the edge of the coffee table. I was just in time to intervene in this minor catastrophe, then eight or maybe ten seconds later the house stopped moving and everything returned to normality.

I made a pot of tea and sat down to consider my world. Life in rock-steady Britain having taught me that the earth beneath my feet was solid and immutable, to find myself living somewhere where it was anything but, I thought in a kind of fatuous, schoolboy-like way, was more novelty than threat.

Earth tremors, even quite severe earthquakes, mud slides and tsunamis are not uncommon in PNG, located as it is on one of the most unstable parts of the earth's crust. Indeed life astride the so-called Pacific Ring of Fire was constant proof of plate tectonics, a reminder that here the boundaries of two continental plates are remorselessly colliding – with, at times, surprising results.

Apart from aggressive snakes and oversized arachnids, one of my other nightmares was to be caught in an earthquake while driving along, and to suddenly see the road open up ahead, swallowing me and my vehicle without trace. Driving in PNG is certainly not for the faint-hearted. Car-hungry gulfs aside, the roads are dusty, potholed, often precipitous and subject to landslides, avalanches, tribespeople, stray pigs, hens and dogs. It was not uncommon to see a vehicle that had failed to negotiate a bend and planted itself in a tree beside the highway. The crucial point here, apart from the obvious one of trying to stay on the road, was of course not to hit a pig, and incur the wrath of whose loss it was.

Whereas British drivers have traffic jams that take so long to negotiate that they need a haircut afterwards, and speed cameras that dispense tickets that beat the offender home, PNG drivers have choking dust, flying stones, timber bridges of questionable pedigree, and dizzying roads unprotected by prissy crash barriers. Instead of traffic wardens there are village big-men who magically appear from nowhere to demand outrageous compensation for the small part of road a driver has momentarily parked upon while taking a pee.

Driving in the Highlands does have something in common with Britain – the roads have similar potholes. The PNG driving experience is further coloured by Hymac drivers who try to knock vehicles off the road with the bucket arm, and wagons that loom alarmingly head-on out of dust plumes.

Considering all the difficulties and hazards of driving in this ludicrous country, I find it nothing short of miraculous there are not more accidents. Consider how a driving licence is issued, for instance. In any other country an intense course of instruction is followed by theory exams and finally a proficiency test. For a driver to qualify in PNG the learner must report to the local police station. Here a police officer stands beside the road and satisfies himself that the applicant can move the car forward a few yards, then do the same in reverse. It does not matter that the vehicle is a total write-off with no mirrors, brakes, or working lights, or in some cases even lacks a windscreen. If it is raining (most days), the testing officer wisely never leaves a sort of serving hatch in the station wall, from behind which he observes the learner driver, in a cloud of blue smoke and a crunching of gears, lurch back and forth a few times.

Hoping not to meet a recently 'qualified' driver with only half a car, I decided to take a run down to the Baiyer River, a valley situated some 34 miles from Hagen, about 1,500 feet lower than, and to the north of, the Wahgi. After its confluence with the Jimi the Baiyer becomes the Yuat, and finally the mighty Sepik, the famous headhunters' river flowing into the Bismarck Sea.

As well as a cattle breeding research station, I had heard that there was a wildlife sanctuary set in virgin rain forest, where crocodiles, tree kangaroos, possums and many species of exotic birdlife could be seen. In fact this reserve probably provided the only opportunity of seeing the fabled bird of paradise, which in its natural habitat is shy, and more often heard than seen.

The sanctuary was about a two-hour drive from Hagen along back roads via a place called Rugli. I packed some lunch, checked the levels of the Toyota and, like good motorists the world over, kicked the tyres. At least I had some brakes and a windscreen, and was capable of moving the vehicle more than a few yards either way. I was off before much of the town was stirring.

It was a fine morning, full of promise, gloriously sunny with the bush still steaming from overnight rains. I was warming to the journey, my first proper adventure since arriving, so I was looking forward to something wild and new. New I could cope with, but I was not prepared for how wild the day's events would eventually prove.

The road was full of craters, so I had to be constantly alert, forever swerving to avoid them and other pitfalls, as well as small groups of tribesmen who were already on the move. Stones kicked up by the wheels bounced off the underside of the truck and spun off into the scrub beside the road. A flock of colourful birds passed overhead just ahead of me. It was a wonderful day and I was thankful to be on the move.

An Eye for an Eye

Not long after leaving Rugli the road started wending its way down the side of a precipitous, forested gorge carved out by the aggressive head-waters of the Baiyer, where it divides the Mount Hagen massif from the Sepik-Wahgi divide, a range forming the northern bastion of the Wahgi

Valley. The rock hereabouts was friable, and the road was prone to frequent landslides.

I had just changed down for the steep descent, when I lurched around a bend to be confronted by a handful of dusty people loitering beside the road. A few rocks were scattered about. I slewed over and got out to investigate.

Some women, a man and a child were moaning and bleeding, and it was obvious that one of the women had either dislocated or broken an arm. I assumed that there had been a car accident; in fact although I was not to know it at the time, the vehicle had left the road and plummeted into the depths of the canyon. There were no other vehicles to be seen. One thing was evident; the people needed medical attention. I had no first-aid kit with me, but offered to improvise a splint to immobilize the injured limb. I would take them all back into town for the medical attention they clearly needed.

'*Yupela mas go long haus sic long Hagen,*' I said with due concern.

'*Nogat,*' replied the man in the

The Victoria Crowned Pigeon (*Goura victoria*) is the largest of its kind in the world

group. He was wearing greyish coloured leaves tucked into what appeared to be a woven hairnet, and stuck behind both ears, rather as a macho construction worker might wear a part-smoked cigarette, was a spatula-like piece of bone. As with men everywhere he was carrying the obligatory axe.

'Yes, *haus sic,*' I repeated with some gravity.

'*Nogat tru. Mipela go long ars ples bilong mi,*' he replied emphatically. '*Yu bai kisim mipela i go.*' This seemed more a demand than a request. With my limited command of Pidgin I was not entirely sure what he was saying, but the gist of it was that they were heading to his village, or some place further down the Baiyer, and I believed he wanted me to take them there. I wasn't altogether comfortable about this. Once again I offered to attend to the injuries, but the man responded almost with an outburst.

'*Yumi go*,' he almost shouted, waving his hand to indicate further down the road. He said something in his tribal tongue to the women who, together with the child, threw in their *billums* and piled into the open back after them. The man's decision became final when he positioned himself beside me in the passenger seat.

'*Go long where?*' I asked, then I enquired if where they were going was a long way.

'*Klostu.*'

Within the limitations of Pidgin it was always difficult to determine such an abstract concept as distance. *Longwe lik-lik* was perhaps best described as not all that close, but not very far either. *Longwe tumas* could be taken as being a very long way away. *Klostu lik-lik* is not as near as just *klostu*. Either way a destination always seemed further than expected.

Resigned to the situation, I drove off. The cab smelled of unwashed flesh, dirt and blood, the overall effect making me feel a little nauseous. We bumped along, with me taking the occasional gulp of fresh air from the open window and snatching glances in the rear view mirror at my passengers in the back.

We had not gone far when we drew alongside a woman heading our way down the road. The tribesman beside me gesticulated to stop. I pulled over and a heated conversation ensued. The exchange was in the Melpa dialect (*ples tok*) but it was unnecessary to understand the tongue to grasp the tenor of what was being said. The woman suddenly began wailing and shaking her arms, pulling at her hair. After five minutes of this we were on our way but very soon pulling over again.

Two men walking towards us solicited a repeat performance, only this time the pedestrians shot angry glances in my direction. Another man abandoned his sweet potato garden, sprinted over and joined in the fray. For the first time I began to worry. Had someone died in the gorge? Were they blaming me for the accident? With growing unease I then recalled the advice of my *haus boi*. An eye for an eye.

There was a noisy exchange between the four men; in the rear of the truck the women and child were whimpering in unison. The conversation by the roadside rose and fell in tempo, with further angry glances for my benefit.

My heart was beating like a condemned man's drum roll, the palms of my hands moist from the tension. At last the three men went their way and my male passenger climbed back in.

'*Orait mipela go*,' he said.

'Go long we?' The man chose not to reply, merely indicated with a wave to keep driving.

Once more I implored the man beside me that we should take the injured to hospital, and yet again the suggestion was rebuffed. We took a side road and headed into the forested foothills, which began pressing in around us. I had no idea where we were, or where we might be heading.

My anxiety deepened with each passing minute.

The valley consisted mostly of tall *kunai* grass that opened here and there onto neat garden plots among which were stands of tall, arching bamboo. Clumps of *pit-pit* sprouted along roadside ditches together with plantains, their pendulous hands of yellowing bananas inviting and luscious. Stately casuarinas[1] overhung the odd trade store where the obligatory 45 gallon drum stood, rusting, and overflowing with garbage.

Rain had started drifting across the valley from clouds that hung like a wet, grey blanket. On my left flank surreal mists were clinging, wraith-like, to grassy spurs that descended to the valley floor like gigantic gangrenous toes. The landscape seemed suddenly dark and threatening.

We had been bumping along now for perhaps another half an hour when a collection of huts appeared to our right. A village. The driver indicated for me to turn in. An eye for an eye – I could not stop this notion crowding my thoughts.

A throng gathered around as I pulled to a standstill. The atmosphere quickly became heated as the injured were all but dragged from the back of the truck. Everyone was highly agitated, some looking in my direction. Matters appeared to be turning ugly. There was much shouting and arm waving. My heart was thumping in my chest as I wondered where it was all leading.

More villagers arrived and further angry exchanges ensued. By this time all thoughts of transporting the injured to hospital were replaced by my increasing concern for personal survival. What really had happened in the gorge? Was I destined to disappear without any trace? It was not fair. This was no just reward for my Florence Nightingale attempts at charity. If only I had heeded the advice. Suddenly an axe-wielding man in traditional dress strode purposefully towards me.

This is it, I thought. Someone, somewhere, will find my remains gathering dust and mouldering in a darkened spirit house. My bones, I thought, would occupy pride of place among someone's collection of ancestral remains, pig jaws and other cultural oddities.

I was almost bracing myself for the transfer to the charnel house, so that it was some seconds before it registered that I was being thanked for my help and repeatedly told I could now go wherever it was I had been heading. Had it all been a misunderstanding on my part? I jumped into the pick-up, all thoughts of bird reserves forgotten. Very soon I was careening at the head of a dust plume along the valley road, anxious to be away from the Baiyer.

Back in Hagen I was shaken to hear that Peter, a local employed by the Autoport, had also been down to the Baiyer Valley that day. More worryingly, he had apparently passed along the same road a few minutes ahead of me, and been stopped by armed tribesmen. With a machete pressed to his throat, Peter had had to talk fast to convince his captors that he had nothing to do with the accident. They released him unharmed but it was a close thing. Hearing this I realized just how dangerous my situation had been. It was a salutary lesson.

A *Dubu* Too Far

Cannibalism was one of the things that fascinated me most about PNG. The consumption of human flesh has been practised in many parts of the world, not just in the Pacific region. Some people might be surprised to learn that even the Celts who colonized Britain and parts of western Europe in the early Iron Age were avid headhunters and, for trophies, hung the severed heads of enemies from their horses, bridles.

Cannibal tribes throughout PNG have eaten people for a number of reasons. The Biamis, of the remote Nomad Region of Western Province, were cannibals because of the scarcity of protein in their impoverished land; they simply hated wasting good food. Some, such as the headhunters of the middle reaches of the Sepik River, killed and

An Eastern Highlands warrior sporting a pig's tusk through his nasal septum and a parrot feather head-dress

ate their foes because they needed heads with which to dedicate each main support post of a newly constructed spirit house.

Others wanted to gain the strength and valour of their warrior victims, or were merely following the rules of the 'pay-back' culture. If, for instance, an enemy had killed and eaten a member of one tribe, the latter would feel obliged to exact revenge in kind. An eye for an eye in its most extreme form. For others cannibalism was more ritual than necessity. The Foré people, for example, followed the macabre practice of burying dead relatives and a week later digging them up and eating them as a sign of respect. Some New Guinea cultures, however, absolutely abhorred the notion of consuming human flesh.

The most famous instance of cannibalism took place at Easter in the year 1901. On that occasion London Missionary Society members the Revds Oliver Tomkins and James Chalmers, together with about ten Kiwai islanders, were invited to *be* dinner at Dopima village on

The undulating back country of the Foré people, the land of 'laughing death'

Goaribari Island, a miserable mudflat between the Kikori River and the Turama delta.

When the LMS schooner *Niue* dropped anchor off the island on Easter Sunday it was immediately surrounded by dugout canoes full of decorated and truculent warriors. They repeatedly invited the white men to their village. Chalmers agreed to go the next morning, when he hoped they would have calmed down, but he tried to prevent his friend Tomkins from accompanying him.

When the two missionaries went ashore the next day the experienced Chalmers must have realized what they had stumbled into. The villagers had recently completed a new *dubu*, or men's house, the construction of which was always dedicated with heads freshly taken from their owners. If no enemy was willing to donate his, then that belonging to any handy friend would do just as well. The two were enticed into the *dubu*, but with hundreds of warriors pressing in behind them, retreat was by then impossible. The victims were clubbed and speared, their heads removed and the bodies subsequently dismembered, cooked with sago and eaten.

When I first heard about the mysterious Foré people and their gruesome eating habits my interest was piqued. Numbering about 14,000, they are confined to the lower montane forests of the Eastern Highlands, in a region delineated by the Lamari River in the east, the Yani to the west, and the Kratke Mountains in the north.

The Foré have always been regarded as a sinister people, feared as sorcerers, untrustworthy, treacherous and practising cannibals. Knowing this I was determined to spend some time with them. I wanted to know whether they still considered relatives a gourmet dish, and I longed to travel where tourists never go, somewhere completely removed from the beaten track.[2] The fact that the Foré are the only people in the world known to suffer from an ailment known as 'laughing death' was an additional peculiarity that attracted me to this backwater of the Eastern Highlands.

I set off at the first available weekend. I was beside myself with anticipation. Between the Wahgi Valley and the Eastern Highlands is the rugged Simbu, a spectacular province of limestone mountains, dashing rivers and waterfalls, ridge top villages and mysterious underground caverns. Overland travel here is challenging.

To reach the town of Goroka, springboard for Foré country, I had first to negotiate the sinuous Daulo Pass, where the dirt road reaches an altitude of a little over 8,000 feet. At this height the Highlands Highway enters the cloud forest, where clammy mists regularly obscure the view and everything is festooned in dripping mosses.

As I crested the pass a fine drizzle veiled the landscape. The road passed through a cutting with 6 foot high clay banks. On top of these I noted a few forlorn screwpines, their spiny fronds stark against the mountain mist, the dead leaves, brown and dripping, hanging limp beside the trunks. Then I began the long, shuddering descent towards the Asaro Valley and Goroka. The Asaro is home to the famous Mudmen and the town has evolved from a tiny government outpost, established there in the 1950s, into a busy commercial hub with a population of around 25,000.

From Goroka a network of bush roads radiated out to Bena Bena, Lufa, and through the heart of the Kratke Range and beyond, where I was bound. Midway between the Simbu border and the Kukukuka country was the Okapa administrative sub-district, where I hoped to find a Foré village friendly enough to allow me to stay a couple of nights or more.

Once the main highway was left behind the route degenerated into a vague artery, where the difficulties of driving multiplied with every turning. Bailey bridges were replaced by timber ones whose reliability was inversely proportional to the amount of creaking. These I crossed with a certain trepidation, but thankfully they hung together long enough.

Oases of dense forest filled the dells and ravines which sometimes separated the hills and switchback ridgelines. The sun blazed overhead. My skin was leaking uncontrollably, the dust adhering to every inch of my clammy body. I had to repeatedly wipe salty perspiration from my eyes. When the track chanced close by the jungly hollows, birdcalls rang out, a haunting sound as if from another world, which I suppose in a sense they were.

When conditions allowed, I would strain against the strong sunlight and peer out at the slow progression of the undulating landscape. It was easy to believe I was watching a three-dimensional cinematograph in which, unbidden, a character would pop up into the scene. It might have been a man standing by a distant clump of plantains or what appeared to be a family group leading a few swine.

After two hours at the wheel I arrived at a village that looked ideal. By this time I was covered in a comprehensive patina of white dust, had biceps like a Sumo wrestler and eyes like organ stops from the effort of concentration. I was definitely in need of a break. The village consisted of a collection of beehive-shaped houses made from woven walls with a pleasing herring-bone pattern. Each was thatched with *kunai* grass, the roof finished off at the apex with a kind of topknot.

I pulled up and a gaggle of children quickly surrounded the Toyota. All had a threadbare look about them. '*Apinun ol*,' I greeted them with a smile.

'*Apinun, masta*,' they shouted, waving and hopping up and down.

'*Bigman bilong ples i stap or nogat?*' I enquired, receiving in response a confused babble as all the children began jabbering together. As more villagers began appearing one of the younger boys ran off, no doubt spreading the word that a *tetegina* (white man) had arrived.

The place had an earthy, back-to-nature sort of smell about it. Hens were cluck-clucking about in the impoverished ground between the houses. As I got out of the pickup I noticed to one side a sad-looking cassowary shoe-horned into a wooden cage far too small for it. A hound was half-heartedly chewing something unrecognizable.

Shortly the boy returned with the village headman. He was unable to speak Pidgin, but through the youngster I learned that his name was Keruma, and that the village was called Perusa, Puroso or something similar. Keruma was a short man with a beard and hair that was turning blond. It was difficult to gauge his age – fifty I guessed – but he was a healthy-looking specimen with arms rippling with muscles. He greeted me with a toothy grin, and a handshake that practically ripped my arm from its socket.

My friend Keruma, a confessed former cannibal from the Foré country

Decorated woman from the Western Highlands. The face pattern is known as 'furrow made by falling tears'

Again through the boy, I explained that I had travelled all the way from Mount Hagen because I was interested in their culture. Would it be possible for me to stay with them for a few days? It was not a problem, the boy told me, after translating.

At first I wondered about the absence of women and teenage girls, but the reason for this became clear later in the day when they returned from tending distant gardens. Indeed, because all their waking hours are thus employed very few, if any, women ever leave their tribal lands, to go to Goroka for instance, and they had therefore never before seen a *tetegina*.

Suddenly I became a celebrity, mobbed by women young and old. My hair was pulled, my arms and legs stroked: an older woman pinched my skin, perhaps to determine if I was substance or *masalai*. In many first contacts between Highlanders and white men, the latter were, because of their pale skin, believed to be returning spirits of deceased ancestors. This notion usually lasted only briefly, for once they realized that the interlopers were mere mortals like themselves, subsequent meetings quite often degenerated into violent confrontations.

I was shown along a trail through some sweet potato plots, to where a clear brook was babbling through a nearby dell overhung with trees, their boughs decorated with arborescent ferns. The creek had a lovely deep pool where I could bathe and wash away the grime of the journey, watched by an ever-changing audience of inquisitive children.

Spam vs Brains

As evening drew its cloak about the hamlet I was spreading out my sleeping bag, and sorting my belongings in the hut Keruma had kindly allowed me to use, when I had the distinct feeling of being watched. I could hear whispering and the occasional faint giggle. Looking up at the walls of the hut, my eyes alighted on a chink in the walls. Here an eyeball was clearly scrutinizing my every move. '*Rouse*,' I shouted, clapping my hands explosively. With squeals of delight the children beyond the wall scattered.

My thoughts once again turned to cannibalism. In the case of the Foré, eating people was a sign of respect for deceased family members. Like her Western counterpart the cannibal housewife took great care preparing meals. The deceased was usually dismembered in his or her own garden using axes and bamboo knives. The hands would first be removed, then strips of the leg and arm muscles, before the torso was opened and the internal organs extracted. Following decapitation the brain would be extracted and everything cooked with vegetables. The meat was usually eaten half raw, but nothing went to waste. Even the maggots were considered a delicacy.

A study of Laughing Death (known as *kuru* to the Foré people) by Dr Vincent Zigas and Dr Carleton Gadjusek in the 1950s and 1960s revealed that a high percentage of sufferers were women. Curiously, the best parts of any cannibal feast, the brains, were usually reserved for the women of the village. Did this have any bearing, I wondered, on the fact that *kuru* afflicted more women than men?

The travel author Paul Theroux, in *The Happy Isles of Oceania*, wrote that all former cannibal cultures of the Pacific had become Spam eaters. Apparently in the absence of human flesh Spam was highly regarded, as being the nearest in taste to the porky flavour of 'long pig', as the cannibals of western Melanesia were wont to call cooked *Homo sapiens*. If Spam was unavailable then corned beef was an acceptable second best. I had noticed throughout all my travels so far in PNG that there was always plenty of corned beef to be found in trade stores. Here with the Foré I was interested to know whether there was still any cannibalism around, or whether they had all converted to tinned meat. I had not seen any sign of packaged meat, so if Theroux's supposition was correct, perhaps they were still enjoying the real thing when available.

Just after dusk that first evening, I was contemplating the rations I had brought with me when, to my surprise, a young woman with a baby in her arms brought me some dinner. The fare, I found with relief, was a large tin of pilchards in hot chilli sauce poured over an enamel plateful of boiled sweet potato. Not the most inspiring of meals, but as I turned in that first night, with indigestion, I took comfort from the fact they ate only family members. Or so I hoped.

Early next morning after a breakfast of more *kau-kau* and spicy pilchards, I took Keruma to one side and through my young translator asked him outright if his kinsmen still ate people. I learned that the practice of burying the dead for a week before eating them had been rare in the southern Foré territory, but more commonplace among their close neighbours beyond the Wanevinti mountains to the north.

He told me his father had practised cannibalism but that it had been stopped by the Government. Though he claimed it was no longer prevalent, I thought I caught a twinkle in his eye.

I decided that there was little to be gained from attempting to explain the possible link between eating corpses and the horrific disease to which they were subject. Besides, others had no doubt tried. In many New Guinea cultures everyday events, mishaps, diseases and the like were ascribed to witchcraft. The Foré were no exception, and many firmly believed that *kuru* deaths were the handiwork of sorcerers with a malicious bent.

I spent the remainder of the day exploring, and visiting other villages in the immediate neighbourhood. Typical hamlets consisted of up to a dozen or more huts occupying clearings hewn from the forest. For defence, these would invariably be sited upon ridges or hill tops. They were once defended by stockades, but these had been pulled down at the behest of missionaries. It was the men who cleared the forest to create gardens, but it was the responsibility of the women to tend and harvest the crops and, as everywhere in the country, to raise and look after the pigs. Everywhere I went, the answer to my question was the same: no cannibalism. I sensed that many of the Foré resented government interference in their customs.

Back in 'my' village, with yet another bowlful of sweet potato and chilli fish, the younger children showed little sign of leaving me in peace. My hut was different from the others, perhaps a former *Kiap* (government patrol officer) rest house, of square construction and set upon 3 foot wooden posts. As a result, many of my admirers' heads only reached to about threshold level.'

'*Mi laik slip nau*,' I said, addressing a row of heads hopefully, '*Yupela mas go long haus bilong yu. Lukim yupela behain* (see you tomorrow).' As with children anywhere there was some giggling, and some pushing. Someone kicked a village hound for no reason, but no one showed any signs of leaving. I decided to hit the sack anyway. Ten minutes later, in the dark, and shrouded in the blankets they had kindly provided, I peeped out from beneath a weary eyelid. My young friends had melted into the night.

Next morning I was awakened by the sounds of giggling and barking. I lay there for some time, listening to the village hens scratching optimistically in the dust beneath the hut. I could detect wood smoke and in the distance hear someone beating one of the hourglass-shaped *kundu* drums.

After a breakfast of, yes, more *kau-kau*, thankfully this time without the pilchards, Keruma gave me a guided tour of the village environs, catching me with my defences down in the process. He turned to me and said something unintelligible. The interpreter boy who had been shadowing us was now grinning from ear to ear, looking furtively from me to Keruma and then back to me as if seeking some reaction.

'OK,' I said. '*Mi no savvi ples tok. Keruma tok olsem wanem?*' There was a brief silence while the boy seemed to be considering the import of what had just been said. I asked again what the old guy was talking about.

'*Yu bai stap long hap na groim kopi.*' He paused to glance again at the village elder then. '*Na supos yu laik kisim meri bilong yu, em i orait.*' What Keruma had just proposed took me by complete surprise. I believe they thought I was very wealthy, a label they probably attach to all Europeans – not that they saw many – because he was inviting me to live in the village. He was even offering me a wife and land on which to grow coffee. He failed to say I would have to buy the land, but I suspected that this would be the case if I accepted. Just exactly what I might be expected to give as a bride price I could not imagine.

He accompanied me on a survey of all that would be my domain should I choose to accept his unusual offer. It would consist of a parcel of land about the size of my garden back in Hagen, perhaps a 1,000 square feet. It was surrounded by a split timber fence and currently had sweet potato crops growing on it, so whether someone would have to be evicted to resettle me I could not say. Of course I declined their kind offer without having the opportunity of meeting my potential bride.

For most of the remainder of the day I played games with the village children. They were fascinated by some of my belongings, in particular my Swiss army knife and a denture with four teeth on it. Afterwards I went for a walk along some paths in the immediate vicinity, marvelling at their neatly laid out allotments.

Though their subsistence lifestyle was based on pig rearing and the sweet potato was their staple, sugarcane, pumpkin, taro, banana and yams were also grown, along with various legumes and root vegetables. They seemed to have everything they needed in life. The encroaching forests were the abode of the *masalai*, but here in the tangle of wild ficus, southern beech, bamboo and pandanus were to be found building and weapon materials, edible fungi and shrubs, bird plumage for *sing-sings* and additional protein in the form of possum (*cus-cus*), tree kangaroo (*karpul*), reptiles, insects, small birds and grubs.

Market in the Eastern Highlands town of Goroka

During my perambulations I met individuals going about their everyday chores. One woman was toting the largest *billum* I had ever seen. She was of course bare-breasted and unshod, her feet the size of coal shovels. '*Apinun, wantok,*' I said, offering the normal greeting, as much from friendliness as to give the woman conversation and a welcome respite from carrying her burden.

'*Apinun, masta,*' came the shy reply without putting down her load.

I looked at the latter and made a conservative guess at almost a 100 pounds. It was then I heard the whimpering. Peering inside the bag I was surprised to find an infant secreted among the unwashed root vegetables. I enquired the child's name. She came over all coy, whispered something I failed to quite catch, then shuffled off along the path. I thought she was blushing, but this was difficult to determine.

A little way further along the way dense *pit-pit* grass, easily 8 feet high, was pressing in to form a living green barrier on both sides of the trail. There was a grunt as a large sow broke cover, startling me. The pig crossed the path seemingly in a single bound to disappear as quickly at the other side. I could distinctly hear it grubbing around somewhere close by. It was time to head back.

On the way I reflected on the past, and how easy it would have been for hostile tribesmen, eager for some 'long pig', to spring an ambush along this muddy native pad. The first I would know of an attack would be when, with a force equivalent to the kick from a mule, the barbed arrows would strike home, or perhaps in the split second of understanding between hearing the rustle of grass and my skull caving in from the blow with a stone club.

As I laboured the remainder of the way back to the village my ears were attuned to the slightest sound coming from the shadows beside the path. The sun was sinking quite low by the time I arrived, panting, back in the settlement. My arrival coincided with much whooping from village children, who appeared to be playing some game involving a living butterfly attached to a stick. An emaciated village cur was howling encouragement.

I caught sight of Keruma crouched outside his house. I sauntered across and saw he was putting the finishing touches to a new axe handle. I thanked him and his people for their hospitality. I commented on his handiwork: for sandpaper he was using the leaves of *selat*, a potent stinging, nettle-like plant that had rough, warty leaves. Through my young translator I explained that I would be leaving the next morning, to which the old man responded by clucking his tongue.

Recrossing the Daulo Pass the next day. I wondered about my hosts of the past few days. I recalled what one missionary is reputed to have said, that cannibals make the best of friends once they have promised not to eat you. My mind's eye flashed one more time upon Spam eating and the age-old traditions of family cannibalism among the Foré people. I had a distinct feeling I knew which they would prefer.

3 Plumes and Arrows

No one knows for sure when exactly pigs were introduced to mainland New Guinea – about 60,000 years ago, with the first people to arrive from South-east Asia seems to be the best educated guess, based on archaeological evidence.

Although the first arrivals were hunter-gatherers, early evidence suggests that by the time people arrived in PNG the pig was already an integral facet of Melanesian economy, and a mainstay of their sophisticated culture. And in a high-speed world of gene manipulation, deep space exploration and high-tech warfare, I found it refreshing to be travelling among people where the bow and arrow is still the weapon of choice, fear of sorcery is high and a pig equates to more than simply a bag of pork scratchings.

A few weeks after I had averted marriage to a Foré belle, rumours of a major pig exchange came to my attention. Since these creatures have become the principal bargaining chip in anything from bride price payments to settling pay-back disputes, any function involving them, I thought, would almost certainly be a spectacle worth seeing.

A few discreet enquiries revealed that a traditional Gawigl-speaking[1] village would indeed soon be throwing a pig-giving shindig. The venue was Wurep, a settlement somewhere due south of Kagamuga within the lee of the Kubors, the lofty mountain range to the south of the Wahgi Valley. Though hardly isolated, or in the remotest sense wild, it would certainly be unique, and in any event my first experience of a traditional *sing-sing*. I was anxious not to miss it.

The day in question dawned like any other in this part of the world, temperatures in the mid-eighties by ten in the morning, the sky an intense cobalt blue. I was under no illusion that it would stay that way, for cloud gathers quickly in these high regions, and despite the dry season there was always the possibility of rainfall as the day advanced. A golden orb spinner (*Nephila maculate*),[2] the large spider whose immaculate web occupied the 5 feet of space between two poinsettia bushes in my garden, was already in position, patiently awaiting delivery of the day's meals on wings.

Packing a few essentials – camera, plenty of liquid, my bush hat, a few cigarettes for trading and also a machete just in case – I donned boots, checked over the engine and half-heartedly swept the previous day's grime from the driver's seat before climbing into my pickup. Soon afterwards the outskirts of Hagen were slipping by amid the noonday heat.

Wiping perspiration from my forehead with the back of my hand, I dropped a couple of gears, and at Kagamuga veered southwards to exchange the Highlands Highway for the suspension-wrecking back country. The alluvial floor of the Wahgi Valley is level hereabouts and, like everywhere in the central Highlands, heavy with cultivation – tea and coffee plantations as well as native garden plots. Either side of the way green sweet potato crops formed quilt-like patchworks contrasting with the rich tilled earth. Clumps of banana and tall stooks of bamboo punctuated the landscape like verdant exclamation marks.

I was travelling on something less than a road. Ahead of me I could see mountains blending seamlessly into delicate shades of indigo, rising like great bulwarks. Cumulus, I noticed, was already gathering on the loftiest summits and spilling forth over sawtooth ridges. The clouds carried a hint of grey, darkening with intent, raising ramparts in the sky. Cheerfully, I bounced along as by degrees my route steadily deteriorated, at the same time luring me ever deeper into the interlocking mosaic of wooded foothills.

Three choices soon presented themselves. Taking the least obvious but what I thought the most likely track, I passed more signs of cultivation. In the near distance to my left I saw women sun-drying coffee on yellow plastic sheets, fanning the beans out with their bare feet. A bearded man was standing by the road-side and I drew up.

'*Apinun, wantok*,' I said, noting with amusement his sartorial elegance – he was dressed in the traditional bustle of green leaves beneath a grey suit jacket. I asked the way and whether it led to the pig ceremony.

'*Em i go stret long Wurep,*' he replied nodding with a stubbly grin.
'*Orait. Tenkyu tru, wantok,*' I said.

'*Supos yu laik kamap long bikpela sing-sing,*' he said, waving roughly in the direction I was heading. '*Dispela rot em i bagarup lik-lik.*' The road was not in good shape. As if to underline this fact the vehicle nose-dived into a mud hole created by recent rains.

The engine almost stalled, the truck wallowing alarmingly as a cloud of steam rose with an angry hiss from the exhaust. In the mirror I could see the old man looking on as I deftly selected first gear and surged forward, building a bow-wave of muddy water ahead. There was a bump as the front wheel rode over a submerged obstruction, and my head struck the door frame making my ears ring. With a final burst of acceleration and a cloud of exhaust I revved the engine and eased clear of the watery trap.

Before long I began to see more people, young and old, heading along the road. There was purpose to their actions. Some were wearing colourful head feathers, others carrying plumes carefully sandwiched for protection between two sheets of bark. Later, with still no sign of habitation, the trickle of walkers had become a constant stream. Everyone seemed cheery, clearly gripped by a carnival atmosphere. It was all gaiety and waves as I chugged by.

A few huts hove into sight. These grew more numerous as I neared my destination, but though the latter remained illusive to the last, the distinctive throaty sound of *kundus* could be just discerned above the noise of the engine. The hypnotic drumbeats were accompanied by an almost primeval chant that, carried on an indolent breeze, rose and fell in cadence.

Rounding a bend, I suddenly found myself at the centre of a long *sing-sing* ground. It was about the size of a football pitch trimmed with natural bunting in the form of neat cordyline hedges, variegated crotons, begonias and pink and red flowering hibiscus. Around the periphery I noticed several thatched dwellings.

Parking the vehicle in the shade of a stately eucalyptus I wandered into the village. People were gathered along the margins of the ground, some seated cross-legged peddling little piles of *buai* (otherwise known as betel nut) or a few sticks of sugar cane. Smoke from village fires was mixing with dust devils kicked up by the pounding feet of enthusiastic dancers. As I cautiously mingled with the throng the unmistakable smell of rancid pig grease assaulted my senses,

vying for attention with the mildly offensive odour of acres of unwashed flesh.

A tourist campaign once described PNG as 'like every place you've never been', and nowhere is this slogan more appropriate than at a traditional *sing-sing*. Laid out before me was a sea of gorgeous head-dresses, a vibrant tide of rhythmically bobbing heads and swaying bird plumage that ebbed and flowed, keeping pace with the strange cantillation. I recognized the florid red tail feathers and canary yellow respectively of Count Raggi and Golden bird of paradise. Additionally I saw the feathers of raptors and owls, those of sulphur-crested cockatoos, complete wings of lorikeets and the whimsical black tail plumage of the flightless cassowary.

PNG is well known for its wood carvings, especially those from the Sepik River. Most Highlands people, however, have little by way of tangible art – certainly no paintings and masks – except piecemeal decoration of weapons and shields. Through these ceremonies they have

Tribesmen dancing a formation known as *Kanan* at a pig-exchange ceremony, Western Highlands

Melpa-speaking tribesman from Togoba village in the Western Highlands. He wears a wig fashioned from human hair, has a pig tusk through his septum and stands next to the 'spirit's eye' at a female spirit cult ceremony

instead elevated self-decoration into a vibrant artform. Their own bodies represent a living canvas, using as a pallet all manner of natural materials: animal fur, bird plumage, leaves and moss, ochre, bamboo, insects, bone and shells.

The way in which these fascinating people paint and decorate themselves follows the patterns of time-honoured tribal tradition. The facial designs and plumage sets reflect their place in society, and through this medium they make social statements, express religious values, or demonstrate their kinship with ancestral spirits of the forest, mountain and underworld.

A man crossed my path, on his head a large black wig made from human hair. It gave to him the appearance of a latter-day Napoleon and was trimmed with, of all things, the live heads of matchsticks. I mused on the effect it would have if one of them was lit. The man was carrying a *kundu*. In Pidgin I asked him what the occasion was. The Pinamby people, he told me, were making good a long-standing debt to their near neighbours, the Kemi Kopelka.

Pigs were of course the currency of the day, and everywhere I looked I saw huge, well-fed specimens. There were pigs on leads, their eyes ringed with red paint, tethered to stakes hammered into the bare earth, restless pigs, shifting nervously against their leashes, large pigs, small ones and noisy pigs.

'*Na dispela sing-sing callem wanem in ples tok* (What is the ceremony called?),' I asked.

'*Ol i callem moka. Em tasol* (It is a *moka*. That's all).'

The *moka*, I was later to discover, is probably the single most important social function in the Highlander's calendar, a colourful pageant practised from the mid-Wahgi through to the Huli people of the Tari basin, in the Southern Highlands. Its central theme revolves around the notional wealth of a village big man. Before the coming of Europeans these ceremonies involved the exchange of thousands of pigs and shell valuables between tribes, clans and individuals.

Rather than having hereditary chiefs, some men in PNG accumulate prestige through their prowess as fight leaders, but most big men achieve social status within their group from the frequency and extravagance of their tokens, nominally pigs and sea shell ornaments, to neighbouring clans and traditional allies. In a sense, *moka* is a bit like a Melanesian equivalent of keeping up with the Joneses.

Though pigs and valuables such as gold-lip shell are the traditional monetary unit, more recently it has also included real money, the kina and toea of commerce. To keep a tally of the alms a big man has given,

Hundreds of beasts tethered in readiness for a pig-giving ceremony in the Western Highlands

Opposite page Western Highlands women dancing *werl* at a pig-giving ceremony in the Wahgi Valley

Left A Wurep tribesman at pig *moka sing-sing*, Western Highlands. He is beating a *kundu* drum and is wearing a human hair wig decorated with bird plumage. Around his neck is a Kina shell and an omak

he wears a pendant known as an *omak*. This comprises a number of parallel bamboo rods threaded onto twine, each strip representing a gift that has been given and, conversely, a favour or gift he is owed in return. By means of this 'ready reckoner', he can easily calculate his accumulated wealth and therefore his status on the social ladder.

A Highland Fling

BOY-ying, *BOY*-ying, went the massed *kundus* as I mingled among the decorated tribesmen. Some, I noted, were carrying intricately decorated stone axes, or frightful-looking spears made from the heart wood of the blackpalm. Although these spears were for ceremonial use only, I had little doubt that if used in anger they could do a great deal of damage.

Dancing a formation known as *Kanan*, a group of Pinamby men formed up in ranks of four or five, chanting and stomping around the clearing. Some held a bow and arrows in one hand, an axe in the other. Others maintained the integrity of their row by each grasping a horizontal spear held out in front of them. To emphasize their masculinity their bodies glistened with pig oil, and each wore a kilt-like brown and white apron from which hung tassels of plaited pig tails.

'*Yu laik baim bo' narrow?*' a man asked, thrusting a fine blackpalm bow and some arrows at me.

'*Nogat.*'

'*Ten kina,*' he whispered conspiratorially as if he was selling off the family silver.

I wavered, examining the arrows closely. Each was made from a *pit-pit* cane. There were two types, some tipped with a broad bamboo blade and others with a hardwood point whittled into vicious barbs as sharp as fish hooks. I asked him what the bamboo arrows were used for. Hunting pigs he told me.

'And the barbed ones?'

'*Long kilim man na meri,*' he said, grinning. These were exclusively used for killing people. I ran a finger thoughtfully over the barbs of one and was convinced of their effectiveness. I handed the arrows back with a final 'No, thank you.'

I had never before encountered anything quite like this. The way these people adorned themselves made them appear not unlike the exotic birds from which they drew inspiration. It gave them an other-worldly

A Mekeo dancer from
Central Province. He is
wearing a dogs' teeth
necklace and a head-dress
of cockatoo, parrot and bird
of paradise plumes

appearance, as if they came from the very paradise from which early sixteenth-century Europeans once believed the bird of paradise originated.

Some of the faces I saw were darkened with pig fat and soot, cheek bones and nose highlighted in red or white. They appeared almost threatening. Wigs were trimmed with leaves, possum fur or sprigs of fern, while a few adult males had curved pig tusks thrust through their noses. I had it on good authority that if they were worn with their points turned down then the owner was friendly, but if they curved upwards the wearer was capricious, aggressive. I noted thankfully that they all had their pig tusks turned downwards.

As I moved around the village the drumbeats thundered and the primitive chanting flowed over me in waves. It was stirring stuff.

I saw pig donors whose finely coiffed wigs were topped with the red tail filaments of Raggiana bird of paradise, or intricate composite feather plaques (*koy wol*). The latter embraced designs fashioned from a collage of red, yellow, white and blue feathers, topped off with those of raptors, as well as the luxuriant metallic blue streamers from the King of Saxony bird of paradise. The overall effect I found quite stunning.

Decorated warrior from the mid-Wahgi valley area of the Western Highlands

Guests from visiting clans could be recognized by their 'second-best' wigs. These consisted simply of a hairnet covering decorated with a few leaves, perhaps a sprig of fern or possum fur, or else a cut-down baler shell, or headband made from either tiny *giri-giri* (cowry) shells or the green carapaces of scarab beetles. I was beginning to feel underdressed in my shorts and tee-shirt.

Cast-off items of Western consumerism are eagerly used to augment the wardrobe of the strutting dandies. Although dried snake skins, plugs of bamboo and pig tusks were the more usual fashion accessories for the ears and nose, it was not uncommon to see villagers wearing ballpoint pens or the side pieces of a pair of spectacles. Once I was amused by an elder wearing a flattened herring can dangling from his earlobe.

Because pig rearing is one of the principal roles of women, they too have an important part to play in the *moka*. Their head-dresses if anything are even more extravagant than those of their menfolk, their faces a vivid red, with nose, eyes and cheeks marked with lines and dots in white, yellow and blue. Groups of older women, usually the wives of a donor 'big-man', form up in lines of three to five, beating *kundus*, and in a dance formation called *werl* lead the singing. 'Look at us, we have raised your pigs,' they chant.

There was a sudden commotion as a large pig broke loose. The mêlée that followed became a hilarious picture of confusion – people dashing this way and that to avoid the hysterical beast, laughing, stumbling, tripping over pig tethers, bumping into each other. Eventually the desperate creature was laid low, stunned, or killed by a single blow to the head with the back of an axe. Afterwards everyone went back to the business in hand, dancing, singing, chewing *buai* and generally having a real Highland Fling.

Although I found the *moka* quite intoxicating, I eventually succumbed to the combined assault of unwashed humanity, the afternoon heat and tenacious flies beyond number. I longed to spend more time with these extraordinary people, but I had to take my leave without witnessing the finale. It was perhaps as well, for the sky by this time had turned to pewter, and as I departed a light but persistent rain began falling. On the way back there was a sudden crack of thunder, as if to emphasize the urgency of returning along the track before escape became impossible.

Gold Fever

By the time I pulled into town the windscreen wipers could barely cope. The sky was divided by powerful streaks of lightning and rain was striking the ground like steel rods, bouncing off the streets to

Wife of a Wahgi Valley village 'big-man'. As a mark of her tribal status she is wearing a lavish head-dress of bird of paradise plumes and a fine baler shell hangs across her chest

create a peculiar ground-hugging mist. I was pleasantly surprised to find that my good friend and fellow explorer, Roy Blackham, had arrived from the UK. Roy was a Mancunian with black hair and blessed with the looks that make women swoon. He had been to the Zagros Mountains of Iran and also participated in an expedition I had previously organized north of the Arctic Circle.

He was one of life's mavericks and a useful guy to travel with: resourceful and loquacious, skills that proved invaluable on more than one occasion. The following weekend I took him on a whistle-stop tour of the Kum Caves and other sights down valley to familiarize him with the local geography. Then we were off seeking our fortune.

Between July 1933 and May the following year two Australian prospectors, Dan Leahy and his brother Mick, had led a prospecting team through the Wahgi and down the Nebilyer into the Southern Highlands, investigating streams along the way. *En route* they chanced on some good colour at Ewunga Creek, and Dan returned later to live at the nearby Kuta Mission and work the find.

Ewunga was near enough for a day excursion and of course the attraction was gold, although our brief time as prospectors was decidedly tongue in cheek. I had recently made the acquaintance of Neil Ryan, a wiry Australian with a ragged moustache which gave him the appearance of a South American gaucho. He worked for the third-level airline Talair, and had lived in-country for some years, previously being employed as a *kiap*. He seemed to know the ropes and offered to find us the tools of the prospector's trade.

Access to Ewunga Creek initially was along the back track to Kuta Mission, from which we branched and followed a switchback trail taking us through the undulating brush country tumbling down from Mount Kuta towards town. Unlike most similar tracks the surface was in reasonable fettle, and we made good progress. Our supplies for the day were stacked in the back of the ute (utility vehicle), including spades and the flat-bottomed, wok-like gold panning dishes that were going to make us wealthy beyond our dreams.

At length we were wading knee deep in a jungle creek as it wound its way through thick undergrowth growing right to the water's edge, Roy dressed in his best denims, Neil and me sensibly wearing shorts and tee-shirts. We halted at what looked a likely spot and began working the alluvial deposits forming the shallow creek bed.

As the day wore on the sun mounted higher in the sky. It beat down

Roy wading down jungle creek on route for the Kum Cave, near Mount Hagen

with unremitting ferocity upon our weary backs as we dug and swirled, dug and swirled the sediment, swishing it around our pans, eyes straining for any hint of colour. The hours drifted by, our eyes popping out of our heads as we scanned the blue-grey sediment, ever hopeful, unfailingly opti-mistic. Dig here. Try there. Anywhere, if only we could unearth a nugget, some-thing at least worth the backache and effort.

Suddenly I wondered who the landowner might be. Wild as this country was, every square inch was the property of someone. Until then it was not a topic to which I had given much thought. But how would the land-owners react to our 'stealing' their gold? I mentioned this to my two companions, who merely scoffed and continued panning.

We had expected at least one nugget bigger than a pin head, but the creek had been worked by professionals. Looking again at the stream bank it was clear that sluicing had once been done there. There was probably no gold remaining. No matter. We had wanted to go gold panning, to do something different, and at the end of the day we had won enough colour barely to cover a finger tip, and received a level of sunburn that would, for a while at least, remind us of our ill-gotten gains.

We called it a day, and amid the first flapping fruit bats and waxing shadows of early evening, went wearily back to where we had left the vehicle. We piled aboard and set off downhill. However, we had gone no more than a mile when we found our way barred by a log laid across the trail. I was immediately on guard, casting anxious glances this way and that, looking for any hint of movement in the dense bush to our right. I was not at all happy. If ever there was an ideal spot to spring an ambush this was it.

'Someone's not keen about us being up here,' I said, looking all around.

'What you on about?' Neil countered as we ground to a standstill. 'It's just a fallen tree, is all.'

'Yeah,' Roy chimed in, with a laugh. 'Just a tree.'

'It's not a fallen tree damn it, it's a log,' I said. Even though we had not found any gold worthy of the word, I expected the sudden zing of arrows any moment.

'Happens all the time,' Neil said.

'Logs don't just fall across tracks,' I urged.

'It's not the 1930s you know.'

'It's been placed there. To stop us,' I said. They would have none of it.

We all climbed out and together heaved the obstruction into the side. 'I've heard it all now,' Roy chortled as we pushed the obstruction out of the way.

I could not help feeling that eyes were watching our every move. But there was no flurry of barbed darts, and much to my relief we continued

Roy and Neil gold panning at Ewunga Creek

unmolested. If anyone had been lurking in the undergrowth then they remained inconspicuous, though in the dense bush at the best of times it was always easy to attach substance to fleeting shadows. Maybe I *was* simply being paranoid after all.

The Mother of Kukumini

The mountain from which Hagen town gets its name rises to almost 13,000 feet, thrusting its lofty summit way beyond the natural tree line. From whichever angle one views it, it is a huge mountain – 100 square miles in extent. It is aligned south–north and separates the precipitous Lai River gorge from the deep trough of the Baiyer Valley.

The Mount Hagen range seen from near town. The dormant volcano Kukumini is in the centre right of the picture

Like other mountains it is regularly hidden beneath a roiling mass of cloud, yet when the weather is clear, usually in the early morning, the bare summit can be discerned rising above its jungle-lagged waistline.

It could clearly be seen from various points around town, and set against the backcloth of its pleated 'skirt' was what appeared to be a flat-topped volcano. One or two pilots *en route* to the Enga confirmed the existence of a crater that marked this lower mountain as an extinct or dormant volcanic vent. The local people knew it as Kukumini.

It was such views of Mount Hagen that over the next few months sustained Roy and me while we were toiling up to our armpits in grime at the Autoport. We thought of it when fitting wing mirrors to trucks with no brakes. It entered our imagination as we built engines from buckets of spares brought in by villagers who claimed that well, yesterday it was working fine. The peak was constantly on the periphery of our vision, overshadowing the town, dominating our thoughts and beckoning alluringly.

When an opportunity arose, we made hurried preparations for an ascent. We did not consider the mountain a major challenge, but for

A colourful Vulturine parrot
(*Psittrichas fulgidus*)

safety and expedience there were some aspects of the climb that demanded careful consideration, not least of which were what equipment to take, and the possibility of altitude sickness. As seasoned explorers we knew that at altitude subtle physiological changes occur within the human body as it attempts to adjust to the rarefied air. If insufficient time is allowed for acclimatization then this results in symptoms that ultimately can be fatal.

We believed that an ascent of Mount Hagen would form an excellent introduction to high-altitude jungle in readiness for a more extensive expedition to the Hindenburg Mountains the following year.

It would be our first sortie into the mid-montane or cloud forest. This is the abode of the reclusive birds of paradise,[3] rare tree kangaroos, *cus-cus*, primitive cycads and a host of exotic flowering plants.

The mountain was 15 miles north-west of town and best approached from the Hagen-Wapenemanda bush road where this slipped ambitiously through the Tomba Gap, and down into the territory of the Mae Enga. We had no guide, nor any cartography better than a teatowel map. We had hopes of finding a way at Tomba that, without too much difficulty, would lead us eventually to the summit. Failing this we had our bush knives.

At 8,000 feet it was perishing at the Tomba Gap, cold enough to wear an extra layer first thing in the morning. We had made a pre-dawn start from town, and the distant Wahgi valley was a sea of early-morning cumulus lapping at the flanks of the distant Kubor Mountains. I drank in the magnificent view. Here and there lofty peaks thrust their tops into the tentative, first light of day.

From the pass we picked up a vague, boggy trail, more a hesitant brush stroke across a rough canvas of muddy sumps and low, moraine-like mounds supporting tussock grasses and a few stunted and gnarled trees. The latter appeared lifeless; indeed many of the trees looked blackened and spent, as if they had in the recent past been ravaged by fire. It later transpired that this and a few other areas at comparable altitudes had suffered severe frosts a few years earlier.

We approached the forest, which looked like an impenetrable green wall. Shortly we came to a stockade made from roughly adzed lumber. We crossed this on a 'stile' of inclined timbers that had steps half-heartedly scratched into them. Beyond was an impoverished group of huts. The children were filthy and snotty-nosed, the adults sullen and furtive, the gardens unkempt and the houses in a parlous state. Hounds scurried out of our way. There was nothing remotely attractive about the place or its inhabitants, so we pressed on silently, without even a backward glance. Isolated *pandans* with crowns of dead and torn fronds stood like oversized tatty feather dusters planted between the settlement and the forest.

Shortly we came to a creek spanned by a rickety bridge. We crossed the suspect bundle of poles, and found ourselves at the feet of the forest. The boughs of the trees, we saw, were bearded with straggly grey-green mosses giving them a superannuated look. After a few more strides we were swallowed by the living turmoil, absorbed into the stifling, muted world of the cloud forest we had heard so much about.

To begin with we made good progress, soon gaining height. It was canopy forest with an under-storey comprised of myrtles, several species of rhododendron and aborescent ferns of all sizes, together with mosses and many unknown shrubs and plants that contrived to impede movement. We trudged on entranced.

Every rock and boulder, every tree, dead or alive, was festooned with filmy lichens and lagged in deep-pile moss, the forest floor itself a depth of decaying leaf mould. This living mantle, we noted, had the identical muting effect on sounds that freshly fallen snow has on a landscape. A single bend in the trail was quite sufficient to muffle a call, to dampen the sounds of feet sloshing through the ooze.

With increasing difficulty we slipped and slithered up mossy banks and over prostrate, decomposing trees. As I negotiated one fallen wood giant, I caught a precious glimpse of a ghostly white butterfly fluttering by on wings sporting large false eyes. Then there was another, and we watched, mesmerized by the sight of these delicate creatures abroad in such a harsh environment. The forest floor itself was a microcosm supporting innumerable communities of invertebrates – insects, centipedes and spiders.

We trekked onwards and ever upwards, the trail growing steeper with every step. Sometimes we were climbing almost vertically through the trees, hauling ourselves up by roots, saplings, anything to help us progress a few more precious feet.

The forest had a smell redolent of freshly dug humus. We were frequently frustrated by the jungle mud, the climb degrading into a three-up two-down arboreal dance routine, making progress very slowly, like going up a down escalator. The trees, too, seemed determined to frustrate our efforts by shooting out their lateral root growths so that we were forever tiptoeing through a treacherous cat's cradle of woody serpents, waiting to wrap themselves around any carelessly placed foot.

Eventually, as if some unseen demarcation line had been passed, the forest suddenly changed, with an increasing preponderance of stilt-rooted screw pines. These *pandans* strode many-legged through an undergrowth that in places became a nightmare of tenacious climbing bamboo, an impenetrable screen that repelled our machetes. The trail, a hunting path perhaps, was vague in the extreme and clearly being reclaimed by the rapacious growth.

An adult cassowary of the deep forests. One kick from its claws can disembowel a man

Apart from the occasional splash of colour from an exotic plant – an orchid perhaps – the daytime New Guinea jungle is in many respects a disappointing place. It was surprisingly silent, too, in a way I found unsettling in a tropical forest. PNG is so unlike Asia, in that it lacks the chatter of primates or the growls, barks and blundering footfalls of larger game animals. Instead the mammals follow the Australian model, marsupials of mostly nocturnal habit, shy and reclusive.

Apart from the querulous peep-peep of secretive skinks and the electronic buzz of a myriad insects, the only sound was our own laboured breathing and the splashy padding of our booted feet along the trail.

Someone once said that releasing me into the wild is rather like letting a bluebottle out of a jam jar. I find it hard to sit still, physically taxing, soporific even to walk at anything less than my optimum pace of 3 miles per hour. I have a tendency to stride off quickly for several minutes, then take a short breather before repeating the process. So I soon left Roy behind. Once when he caught up, Roy told me how I could be seen disappearing around bends in the trail, or into green hollows, to reappear again hopping over dead trees and skirting mossy boulders. My habit of moving fast then halting briefly, before moving off again, gave my movement a staccato-like appearance.

Once when together Roy and I were taking a well-earned breather, we had the good fortune to spot a ribbon-tailed astrapia,[4] the wavering white streak of its 3 foot long tail streamers marking the wraith-like passing of this secretive bird, as in swooping flight it silently passed between the crowded boles. This sight alone, we agreed, made the climb worthwhile.

Out in front once again, my route levelled off briefly before turning slightly downhill to meet a jolly stream. By this time I was thirsty and tried taking a draught without first removing my backpack. This was a mistake. While down on all fours my pack shifted momentarily, pinning my head under water. Spluttering, I shrugged off my load in disgust before taking several gulps more, at the same time observing movement in the nearby leaf litter – a shiny black millipede.

Hefting my pack I strode off as a 'wauk-wauk-wok-wok-wok' sound echoed hauntingly through the trees. Hurdling yet another fallen tree I missed my footing. Automatically extending a hand to save my balance, I narrowly missed grasping a slender palm-like plant. The trunk, the leaf stems, and even the leaves themselves, were all liberally endowed with lethal-looking, 2 inch spines that would most surely have penetrated right through my palm. I cursed the log before continuing.

Several more streams crossed our path, in most cases flowing unseen through jungly gullies that were a tangled confusion of dead trees and thick undergrowth. At one ravine a fallen tree had formed a convenient bridge. Since the alternative was ten or fifteen minutes thrashing down into the purgatory of the hollow, followed by a sliding blunder up the far side, I opted to chance the crossing in a slow, deliberate shuffle.

It was at this point that I noticed the woefully inadequate state of my 20 kina boots. I had purchased them from one of the local trade stores just a few days before, but they were now, I noted with alarm, already coming apart. This was potentially serious.

With altitude, the canopy lowered, and the trees thinned out to be replaced by a wiry, birch-like shrubbery. Additionally there was a higher proportion of tree ferns (cycads). Neither trees nor ferns, this species has changed little in over 290 million years.

Striding triumphantly clear of the tree line at last, we entered a moorland realm of snow grasses, ericas, gentians and other alpines. Our altitude was by then reading about 11,000 feet. At this height the primitive cycads had multiplied exponentially. They were everywhere, striding up the higher slopes and drifting over the landscape into grassy hollows and dells.

We donned our waterproofs as a barrier against the damp clouds. It was chilly too, I could feel it seeping into my bones. Vapours raked the upper slopes. Rock bands were there one minute and gone the next, cycads drifted in and out of vision, ghost-like among the grey forms, their spidery fronds forlorn, dripping. Before too long through the clinging damp, a rocky point loomed from where, it seemed, all ways headed downwards again. The summit at last.

We stayed a while on Mount Hagen's misty top, but there was no uplifting panorama on this, our very first New Guinea summit. Nevertheless, we congratulated each other on a fine effort, and lingered to take sustenance, and briefly nurturing a forlorn hope that against all odds the cloud would disperse to reveal a magical world at our feet. But with no such luck, and with a cheated feeling, we girded our loins and, with an anxious look at my footwear, headed downhill for the reverse slither back to the Tomba Gap.

The Hagen climb had been an invigorating experience. My boots, fortunately, had held together just long enough, but barely had we cleared the mountain than we were each contemplating what our next adventure might possibly be. My first action, however, was to purchase some tougher footwear.

There were other high peaks of course, including the 14,300 foot high Mount Giluwe, several summits in the Kubors and Wilhelm, at 14,793 feet representing the country's highest point. Moreover, there were vast tracts of untrammelled jungle and areas of limestone absolutely riddled with gorges, caves and potholes. As we were soon to discover, though, adventure often came unlooked for and from the most unexpected quarter.

An Encounter with Silkworms

Life in the Western Highlands was not bad. With an altitude a little over 5,000 feet, the year-round spring-like climate of Hagen town was like Utopia. Although midday temperatures regularly reached the upper eighties, the relatively low humidity made the mountain valleys more bearable than the coast, there were few mosquitoes, and the most venomous snakes, the taipan and death adder in particular, were restricted to lower altitudes.

Hagen town enjoyed a vibrant social scene, mostly based on the bar at the Hagen Park Motel and, as we found out, had a sizeable British

Voluntary Service Overseas community. These were all paid local wage rates and covered a wide spectrum of disciplines, from civil engineering and teaching to agriculture. We were introduced to a young fellow called John Brooksbank. With his boyish looks and mop of wavy blond hair he looked no older than his mid-teens. I thought he had one of the more bizarre occupations.

The Government was introducing new cash crops at grass-roots level – tea and coffee were already well established in the Highlands – including what might be termed European vegetables. New industries were the focus of trials, including a cattle breeding station. John, however, was experimenting with developing a silk industry. Just how the authorities thought they might compete with giant producers like China and India I struggled to understand. But like other volunteers in town, John was keen to give it his best shot. He was a likeable sort and invited Roy and me out to his lab to see for ourselves.

From the outside there was nothing unusual about the building housing John's facility. It was like any other structure – prefabricated with louvre windows, corrugated roof, fly screen door – but what set it apart once inside were the numerous glass-topped trays housing thousands of silkworm moth larvae busily champing through their food of choice, the leaves of the *Morus alba* (mulberry tree).

Down both walls were innumerable racks not unlike those used to display postcards. But instead of cards they held countless adult silkworm moths, just perched there, motionless except for the occasional tremor of a wing to indicate they were indeed alive.

A distant Mount Giluwe seen from the Tomba Gap. Giluwe is the second highest mountain in Papua New Guinea at 4,367 metres (14,330 ft)

The *Bombyx mori* moth has a fat white body and pale wings with a nominal span of around 2–2½ inches. Apparently over the thousands of years since China first began producing silk the adult moths have become so domesticated that they are passive and are no longer capable of flight or of feeding themselves. We moved in for a closer look, intending to twirl the racks round. 'No!' John shouted – just too late to warn us about the creatures' unique form of defence.

In the most amazing act of synchronized peeing I have ever seen, they all angled their abdomen in our direction and together drenched us with a vile moth liquid. Driving back home with the windows wound fully down, I suddenly laughed. 'Who would believe it?' I said.

'Well, it's not every day you get attacked by moths,' Roy replied.

As this incident proved, there was little need to leave town to have close encounters of a strange kind. Another example was that nearly everywhere one chose to step from a vehicle the plants growing by the wayside wrapped themselves around your feet. The first time this happened I found it a trifle disconcerting, but after a while I became used to it. It was just one particular species that did it, I never discovered what it was called, but it obviously had some sort of trigger that caused it to close in upon itself. When stimulated each segment of the pinnate leaves would fold itself, then each leaf stem together and finally the whole plant contracted. You could literally hear the plant move, and if your foot just happened to be in the middle of a patch, you found yourself trying to shake it off as you would a Jack Russell terrier. It could be quite spooky.

4 Two Pommies, an Aussie and a Funeral

One of the principal reasons for our presence here was that we were impatient to join a large British expedition to investigate the isolated mountains close to the Irian Jaya border. It was not scheduled for many months yet, and in the interim we were actively training for it, and in the process seeking thrills and exotica wherever they were to be found.

It is hard at first to come to grips with a country as unique as this, but I guess I was starting to like the place when I learned that the Pidgin for a saw was a *push-i-go-pull-i-come*, and that the first elected Prime Minister, Michael Somare, was a Sepik River headhunter's son. When I first arrived I had no real preconceptions. All my research – the books, and the colourful anecdotes – merely served to underscore the exceptional nature of the place.

One microcosm of civility, which coincidentally was also the source of a rather curious encounter, was the town's little bakery. That a one-horse town like Hagen possessed a bakery was a pleasant discovery in itself, but that was not all. Behind the counter was a drop-dead gorgeous, part Filipina New Guinean beauty. I doubt if there was a single male in town who was unaware of Maria, or did not salivate at the mere thought of her smooth latté complexion and superb figure.

Every day Roy went in for a sandwich, and each time he asked for a date. In each instance the answer was always a definite 'No'. Three weeks passed and Roy continued to fish for a date with his lunch. Then out of the blue she said yes. Later he told me what then transpired.

'Where would you like to go?' she asked him. Roy suggested the 'haus flea'.

'Oh, I can't go there.'

'Why ever not?'

'Can't,' she persisted without explaining.

'Hagen Park Motel?'

'No!'

'Stock car racing?'

'Don't be silly.'

'Where then?' Roy finally asked, exhausted of ideas.

'How about your flat?' she offered. After a moment's hesitation Roy said he would pick her up at seven.

'It's fine, I know where you live. At seven then, see you there.'

I was immediately intrigued. I considered making myself scarce, but exactly on cue that evening we heard heavy footsteps followed by a less than demure knock. When Roy opened the door he found filling it a mountain of a man wearing a policeman's uniform, with a sidearm on his belt and a pickaxe handle swinging from one hand.

'You Roy?' I heard the colossus growl. I tried to look inconspicuous.

'I've brought Maria,' he said. 'What time should I come back for her?'

'Eh, what?' I heard Roy croak. 'I think there's some mistake. I didn't realize Maria was your girlfriend.'

'Wife.'

Oh bugger, I thought.

Expecting blood and bone to start flying anytime soon, I was knocked for six by what followed. 'What time do you want me to collect her?' he asked again.

'Er … will eleven do?' Roy stammered. And for several weeks, like clockwork, Maria's very significant other brought her around to our flat, and collected her later the same night. No matter how much I thought about it I was unable to get my head around this and wondered if it was some sort of bizarre time share. Then Maria began dropping subtle hints that she was childless and unhappy.

Then after three months the visits abruptly ceased. It was just another of the unfathomable brief encounters that life in Papua New Guinea kept producing. It occurred to me what a singular country this was, what wonderfully unpredictable people.

Another freakish feature was the power of tropical storms, something that never ceased to amaze. The rain fell so heavily it always announced its arrival with a noise like an approaching juggernaut, as the deluge beat down on the forest embracing the town. From our first-floor flat window we enjoyed almost nightly ringside seats as the night sky hosted spectacular *son et lumière* shows. Lightning would split the firmament wide open, the black clouds inwardly convulsing with flashing stroboscopic images.

The thunder when it came was instantaneous, not the low, rolling suggestion of a distant tempest, but a brain-jarring '*BOO*-ooom' that left us practically shell-shocked. Each unexpected blast would rattle the roof, shake the louvred windows and have us both leaping out of our shoes like nervous wrecks. On occasions during our night-time return journeys from weekend adventures we witnessed as many as four separate thunderstorms dancing around the distant horizon. In pleasant contrast to this incalculable power was the bioluminescence of fireflies twinkling in their thousands like fairy dust in the arboreal shadows beside the road. The two extremes of this display were always a treat for whoever got to ride in the open backed pickup.

Just occasionally the small hours were disturbed by other uncontrolled forces of the night. Once awakened by loud, splintering crashes we wandered over to the window, and saw 'rascals' across the dimly lit street casually axing their way through the walls of a store. '*Pasin bilong Niugini*,' we both muttered sleepily, before shuffling back to our

Thatched branch of the Papua New Guinea Banking Corporation

cosy beds. Next morning as I strolled by, I saw a policeman peering into a hole large enough to drive a motorcycle through.

Faced with a thatched hut marked 'Papua New Guinea Banking Corporation' one day, I wanted to investigate, but to my regret the door was locked, so I was unable to enter, and gawk at the only grass-built bank I can honestly say I have ever seen.

At another, more thought-provoking time and place, I visited a leper colony and was touched by the kindness of the inmates and the unassuming nature of the nuns who attended their needs.

In the virgin rain forests of Baiyer River Roy and I dangled from soaring, buttress-rooted forest giants, and swung, Tarzan-like, on jungly vines not unlike the finest-quality ropes.

Proceeding through the Southern Highlands one day *en route* to the provincial headquarters at Mendi, we noticed beside the road an odd-looking wooden box on a post. It resembled one of those mail-boxes everyone in the USA seems to have at the end of their drive.

Skull box by the roadside in the Southern Highlands

But again it was thatched, and there was definitely no door-to-door mail service.

'What do you suppose that is?' I asked, nodding in the direction of the structure by the roadside.

'Somewhere to leave the newspaper?' Roy replied smiling.

'Milk bottles,' I said.

'High-rise kennel for a small dog with long legs?'

We both laughed. In truth we had no idea, but curiosity got the upper hand. So we reversed back to look it over. When we peeped inside three skulls grinned back at us, their eye sockets blank, unseeing. We did not find this in the least bit gruesome, simply … different.

Why is it that such a sinister aura always surrounds human skulls? In Western countries we do not leave them lying around everywhere, do we? It is hardly normal to keep the treasured cranial remains of deceased relations boxed up with other family heirlooms in a cupboard under the stairs, or displayed along with the coronation souvenir plates on the Welsh dresser. But things are different in New Guinea. Human remains are everywhere. It is an acceptable cultural thing, an inescapable facet of life. Almost any dark hollow or rock shelter will have at least one leering skull. A *haus tamburan* (spirit house, the traditional repository of ancestral remains and other cult objects) might have racks full of ancestral bones. In the Eastern Highlands I once came across a skull mounted on a pole in the former owner's sweet potato garden, left there, I was informed, to protect his crops from evil spirits.

In this context the practice is not so unusual. In a country known for its cannibal and headhunting past one expects to encounter the occasional nest of peppermint-stick bones, or a bleached head or two. In the Eastern Highlands, the Kukukuka like to preserve the whole body of deceased family members, better to enjoy them later. The corpses are usually placed in a seated position on a platform of branches – beneath a rock overhang perhaps, or up a tree – and sun-dried.

The main attractions of this wild land, however, were the inhabitants. Pay-back disputes often spilled onto the town's streets. Although there was never any threat to whites, those of a weaker disposition found such events unnerving and hid away. In the resulting chaos, as hundreds of armed warriors stampeded through the streets, the timid would cower in stores, or lock themselves in houses while arrows careened off parked vehicles or skittered across corrugated rooftops.

In one unforgettable incident a band of yellow-painted tribesmen came swooping through Hagen, spears and axes waving. I decided to follow them at what I imagined was a discreet distance, hopeful of some dramatic photographs. Parking my Mini Moke on the southern side of town, and proceeding on foot, I slinked nervously from street corner to street corner, trying to keep one step ahead of my quarry while anticipating their movements.

I waited expectantly, camera at the ready. I could hear shouting as the tribesmen passed along the next street across from where I stood. Then there was a sudden yammering as they swept around the corner of Romba Street, about 150 yards away. There was a forest of axes, spears and bows and arrows waving in the air like the massed dorsal fins of a shoal of ocean predators.

Then, like surf rolling up on a defenceless shore, the mob surged forward, catching me unawares. I was too far from the Moke, and yet even as that thought registered I became aware of a Land Cruiser parked nearby, its engine ticking over. Fortunately it was facing away from the tribesmen.

The warriors were coming closer, weapons waving with menace. An arm was extended from the driver's window of the Toyota. 'Come on, quick,' a voice called. I hesitated, glancing over my shoulder. The warriors were nearer now, spears jabbing the air. So I ran and leaped in, and with a squeal of rubber we shot off. Glancing back I saw my beloved Moke swamped by the rising yellow tide. 'What do you make of that?' I asked the driver, whom I had never met before. He said his name was John.

'Ah, it's all show, mate.'

'You think so?'

'Yeah. Seen it all before. Bushies make a lot of noise and wave weapons around, but mean nothing by it.'

'Show or not I don't fancy being on the wrong end of one of those spears,' I countered.

'Well … yeah, there is that,' John said with a hint of humour.

'Thanks for the rescue, anyway,' I said. I offered to buy him a beer if I bumped into him at the Hagen Park.

'No worries, mate. Where d'ya wanna be?'

'Anywhere'll do. Thanks.'

In the event we drove around the block and returned to Romba Street. The fracas had by then moved safely off down town. He dropped me by the Moke. I expected to find it with its canvas top slashed and spiked like a pin cushion but miraculously it was left unscathed.

Afterwards I convinced myself that there had been little danger. But to stand my ground would have taken more nerve than I had at the time. I once heard a tale of how a white man driving along the main highway had been forced to stop when he found his way barred by a tribal fight. The hostilities ceased momentarily and a warrior sauntered over to cadge a light for his smoke. Once the driver was through, the lines closed up again and the tribesmen resumed hammering seven bells out of each other.

White Man's Magic

In such a geographically convoluted land a lack of accurate maps can be a serious drawback. But in PNG it

Skull of deceased villager 'watching' over his sweet potato garden, Eastern Highlands

was worse than that: there were no charts better than the tea-towel maps one might find in curio stores. This state of affairs, however, rather than being an impediment, was a source of delight to two adventurers like Roy and me. For several months our expeditions would be dictated by our 'tea towel', our tactic being to drive off the 'hem' and just keep on going to see where we finished up.

Once when we reached the end of the vaguest of bush roads, we continued weaving between trees. The jungle soon scotched hopes of driving further, so we halted and walked the rest of the way into a remote little settlement. Roy was always boasting how it was possible to obtain a Coca-Cola anywhere in the world. The village, we noticed, had a curious little trade store so we wandered over to discover what it had to offer. And sure enough, the shelves held bottles of Coke, and were also stacked with tinned fish and meat and, for reasons that escaped us, a human foetus in a pickled egg jar!

At another jungle terminus, we threw down the gauntlet to the finest archers of one tribe. The arrows used throughout PNG are made from *pit-pit* canes, long, shafted and flightless. Though many of the earliest pioneers could testify to the deadly accuracy of these arrows at close range, beyond a few dozen yards they tumble hopelessly out of control and flop to the ground like a wet dishcloth.

Using cut-up cigarette packets as makeshift fletching we adapted several arrows with flights. Taking his time, Roy patiently explained the purpose of this to the fight leaders, showing them how to fashion flights. For our efforts we won their admiration by firing our modified arrows down the *sing-sing* ground, about the length of a football pitch. The whole village, it seemed, had by this time turned out to watch, and our arrows, in every case, flew straight and true. And all the more impressive for it, they landed point first to the accompaniment of much ooh-ing and aah-ing.

When it was the turn of the home team the outcome was wholly predictable. Their arrows covered half the distance, but long before that they were tumbling haphazardly and landing anyhow except point first. Despite this the menfolk entered into the spirit of the competition, whooping and jumping about like spectators at a football match. A full-sized blackpalm bow takes some muscle power to draw fully, but one bowman amazed us by pulling his so far back it actually snapped.

On our return to the village months later we wondered what we might find. Our pupils would have had an unfair advantage over any foes and we half expected to discover that we had been responsible for a quantum leap in the mortality rate. However, we need not have worried for, despite the superiority of fletched arrows, they had continued using their inefficient, flightless shafts.

This would not be our last encounter with armed men. Shortly after our archery tournament we found ourselves once again bouncing along the dusty tracks which formed part of a previous incarnation of the main Wahgi highway. Having turned along what passes for a B road we came upon a jolly band ambling along with enough primitive weaponry to start a war. We pulled over to engage them in banter. With us was a young electrician who that very week had arrived from Australia to work at the Autoport. His name was Mike, and when we announced we were off seeking adventure, he had asked if he could come along too.

As we pulled alongside the warriors Mike's eyes widened like saucers. We asked the tribesmen where they were heading. '*Mipela laik go long ars ples*' ('We wish to go to the village in which I was born') came the reply. There were about a dozen of them. We got out and went through the ritual of shaking hands with each. They seemed a friendly bunch and so we asked if where they were heading was nearby. '*Klostu*,' they said. We offered them a lift and gestured for them to climb aboard. Each had a long blackpalm spear, and they were also carrying their own fire in the form of glowing embers, which naturally we wished to keep clear of the jerricans of fuel in the back. It was not unusual to encounter travellers carrying fire with them.

Despite our pleas for them to be seated, they insisted to a man on standing bolt upright with their weapons pointed skywards. This was a potentially dire situation. The back roads are not good at best, but

Roy and our hitch-hiking warriors on their way to a funeral, their spears pointing skywards

each time we cornered they caused the Toyota to wallow alarmingly, so much so that we feared it might roll into a ditch and kill us all. Roy put his head out the window and called for them to sit. They smiled their betel-stained grins and remained standing.

A mile or two later one of our passengers hammered on the cab roof. We jerked to a standstill and they all leapt out with a noisy air of bonhomie. We watched with interest as they began digging in the banking beside the road, looking for yellow ochre, which they mixed with water from nearby puddles before smearing it all over each other – hair, faces, arms and chest.

'What's all that about?' Mike asked.

'Beats me,' I replied. Roy suggested they were going to some sort of ceremony. That much was self-evident. But what kind of celebration demanded such earthy garb.

'*Mekim wanem?*' I enquired.

'*Wantok bilong mipela em i dai pinis,*' they replied. '*Mipela go long sing-sing. Em i orait supos yupela laik cam up long dispela ples na lukim.*' They were heading for the funeral of a fellow clansman and in return for giving them a lift they were inviting us along to join them as guests. It was the best offer that day and we eagerly accepted.

After the make-up interlude the road became less sinuous and everyone relaxed, except Mike, who was still unsure what to make of our new friends. At length we reached our destination. It followed the typical pattern of Western Highlands homesteads, consisting of a handful of oval-shaped houses. People were milling around. We parked and made ourselves welcome.

Tiggi was like any other settlement in this part of the province; there was no particular reason for its existence. Apart from the ubiquitous trade store, which had walls woven from split cane, the houses were fashioned out of timber planks planted in the ground and lashed in place with rattan. A thatched roof of *pandan* leaves or *pit-pit* completed the structure.

A flue is unheard of in New Guinea house construction, and with no windows either, smoke from the hearth permeates out wherever it can through the thatching. Once inside one of these low-slung dwellings it is preferable to crouch, or crawl about on the earthen floor, risking hookworm, rather than suffer the lung-retching fug gathered above waist height. The smoke possibly helps in keeping fleas and other parasites at bay.

As with most New Guinea villages the focal point was the formal dancing ground. This was overhung by avenues of graceful casuarinas trees whispering in the warm breeze. There seemed to be hundreds of villagers present, milling about trance-like or sitting cross-legged on the dried earth. Dogs were yelping and scurrying about under people's feet.

Greeting people with the usual 'Apinun, wantok', we found a convenient place at one end of the cleared area and sat down to watch the proceedings. Many of the womenfolk, we observed, were wandering around bare-chested and clearly distressed, wailing and vigorously attempting to pull out their hair in lumps. Yellow or white clay had been rubbed into their hair and was dried and cracking on their skin, falling from their breasts like leprous flakes. Each woman had a switch of the cordyline plant with which they thrashed themselves, and each other, while slowly mumbling some unintelligible mantra.

Tribesmen at Tiggi village charge around a *sing-sing* ground during a funeral

Smoke was drifting across the ground from the fires and *mu-mus* no doubt slowly cooking root vegetables, bananas and *abus* (meat) killed earlier. The smoke was irritating our eyes.

Men brandishing axes and uttering an incantation started walking around the dance ground, gradually building up speed. The stroll became a jog, then they were running, bare feet pounding the earth. As they reached the farthest limit of the arena they turned to face our little band, accelerated and charged seemingly straight towards us, holding their axes aloft in what appeared to be a threatening manner. Mike was restless, I noticed, looking for somewhere he could run for cover. As the villagers rushed forward it appeared that they would not make the turning at our end of the ground.

Eyes wide with alarm, Mike sprang to his feet. Roy reached up at the last minute, grabbed him by his belt and pulled him slowly back to the ground. Mike was horror struck, as he watched the warriors on their final approach. At the very last instant the chanting axemen swerved to one side and round again, to begin another circuit.

Perhaps it was a little cruel, since we had some idea what to expect, but both Roy and I were laughing uncontrollably, revelling in the discomfiture of our young companion. His response was a heart-felt 'Pommie bastards'.

We hung around for maybe a further half-hour before thanking our hosts and taking our leave. Just as we were departing we were each handed a lump of pork, steaming fresh from the *mu-mu*, wrapped in banana leaves. We thanked our hosts once again.

I always found New Guinea pigs a little worrying. They seem feral, never quite wild and yet not completely under the domestic yoke. They could grow to immense size, and were mostly hairy. Even cooked they were scarcely wholesome, usually infested by tapeworm. The meat is always fatty and undercooked and for all these reasons very definitely bad news. Once clear of the village Mike unwrapped his banana leaf parcel. The smell was awful.

'You going to eat that?' I asked.

'Are you yours?'

'Not bloody likely,' I retorted, turning to Roy. He was driving and just shook his head. Having put a respectable distance between us and Tiggi we threw our packed lunches unceremoniously into the brush beside the road.

Pigs' Heads and Paw-Paws

Soon after my arrival in PNG I discovered Hagen's excellent local market. Here each Saturday it was possible, for a couple of kinas, to fill a hessian sack with enough fresh produce to last a week or more. A visit to the market was always the highlight of the week in Hagen for it was an excellent place in which to indulge in some people watching.

Since gardening was women's work, they were responsible for harvesting produce, and for selling any surplus. This they did from stalls consisting of low, slatted wooden benches open to the elements, although others, circular in design, had a conical thatched canopy shielding them from rain or sun, both of which could prove powerful beyond reason.

Those women who arrived too late to secure a place at a stall would squat in the dust in small groups hawking sweetcorn, *kau-kau*, sugar cane, whatever little they had to offer. With faces aged by tough years in the garden, they would look on passively as potential buyers cast appraising eyes over their wares. There was never any pressure to buy.

Some of the older women, I noted, had balding strips across their heads, rubbed to the scalp by a lifetime of *billum* carrying. As I strolled casually around I thought how marvellously organized the market place was. Although there was a throng there was no jostling; everything was orderly and there were no florid invitations to buy a bargain that one might hear in, say, a Moroccan souk. The air was sultry, the sun unremitting, and I was glad to be wearing a hat and sunglasses.

One stall had some of the largest bananas I had ever seen. There are sixty varieties of banana; these were cooking ones I was told by the woman selling them. They were fully a foot in length. They were a popular titbit with the locals, and when cooked the traditional way, in a *mu-mu*, usually resembled steamed candles, with about as much taste and nourishment value.

The weekly Hagen fair was always a feast for the eyes as well as the taste buds. Apart from what might be termed European fruit and vegetables, there was always a cornucopia of the unusual and exotic: sweet potato, earth-encrusted taro and other root crops, the bitter-tasting star fruit, milky peanuts, piles of knobbly root ginger, and other

The meat stall at Hagen market – dubious cuts of meat

produce completely alien to me. Some stalls were piled high with sticks of sugar cane and sweet corn, or heaps of betel nut.

I saw green avocados and shiny, red-black egg plants. One stall had just a pathetic handful or two of berries, nearby were a few withering legumes, and some melons at another bench. There were plump pumpkins and paw-paw, apple-cucumbers, runner beans, a few green oranges, and *kumul* (the leaves, stems and tendrils of marrow and pumpkin), which when boiled up tasted not unlike spinach.

The meat stall could be found by following the ubiquitous flies, and had a blackened pig's head, with its snout pointing skywards occupying pole position, with other dubious cuts of meat ranged alongside it. Sometimes there would be a small bird or two, perhaps a tree kangaroo or possum, on offer. Occasionally someone would bring in live specimens, to be tethered by bush rope to a post, or crammed into ludicrously small bamboo cages. I was always sorry for these doe-eyed, harmless marsupials of the high forests.

Like markets everywhere, it was busy, with people quietly haggling, comparing produce and prices from one stall with others. Idling men wandered about in 'arse grass' and *lap-lap*. Women, their necks invariably swaddled in multicoloured trade store beads, strolled by with shoulders wrapped around with cotton in a rich burgundy, extending down to their ankles. All had *billums* suspended down their backs, and gaily coloured armlets woven from the tiniest beads tightly shrunk onto the upper arm.

'How much for the paw-paw?' I asked of a woman with prune-like features.

'Fifty toea,' she croaked. She accepted thirty.

I had tropical fruit salad in mind. And while selecting a pineapple and some passion fruit at a bench I noticed a middle-aged white woman, a brunette, at the other corner bartering for some avocados. I sidled over and struck up conversation. She introduced herself as Terri. Talk shifted from the wide choice of exotic produce and how cheap everything was, to the weather, lazy Hageners and the 'rascal' problem.

'Have you heard about the trouble?' she asked.

'What trouble?'

'*Kanaka* fighting, out along the Baiyer road,' she said. I noted that she used the offensive patois for a tribesman.

'No,' I confessed. She had my full attention though. A tribal fight, I thought. Fighting was officially banned, but with friction caused by over population in the region[1] conflicts were still prevalent, mostly fuelled by land disputes. Women, pigs, pay-back, and nowadays even traffic accidents, were all additional causes of strife. Moreover, the advent of modern weapons and urban migration was starting to exacerbate this lawlessness.

'We were out that way yesterday,' she said, as she pointed quizzically at some yellow stubby objects shaped like miniature zeppelins. 'Do you know what those are?'

'Banana passionfruit,' I said. 'Quite tangy.'

'My husband, David, he's a pilot,' she told me. 'Flies F28s for Air Niugini.'

'Did you see any action then, down the Baiyer road?' I asked as I stuffed a small melon into my bag.

'No, not much, but it's still going on, apparently. Has been for a week or two.'

The Battle of the Baiyer Road

The population of PNG is one of the most heterogeneous in the world, and of the several thousand tribes, most number only a few hundred people. The isolation created by the rugged terrain is so acute that some groups were unaware of the existence of neighbours only a few miles removed until relatively recently.

Divided by extremes of topography, language and customs, some highland clans have engaged in low-scale tribal conflict with neighbours for thousands of years. When government patrols first made contact with many of them warfare was as much a daily fact of life as rainfall. Fighting, cannibalism and head-hunting were among the less desirable activities that the administration had been keen to eradicate. There was some resentment at the interference, and they met with limited success in some areas more than in others. Hagen was a case in point, where sporadic fighting has continued unabated using traditional weapons.

I had never seen a proper tribal fight, with real arrows and spears. *En route* to a pay-back ceremony, hundreds of warriors sometimes marched, painted and fully armed, through town, but this was hardly the same. I was desperate for some dramatic photographs, and hoped to see for myself a genuine conflict close up.

Armed tribesmen rampage through the streets of Hagen township

I made some enquires early the following week. The fighting, I

discovered, was between two long-standing enemies, the Jikka and the Yamuga. What amounted to a running sore between the two tribes had recently flared up once again, and this was the most recent call to arms in a seemingly endless run of battles to resolve ownership of disputed land. I was determined to see for myself. It was a Tuesday. Worried that it would be all over by the coming weekend, I took every available chance, usually with extended lunch breaks, to drive at break-neck speed down the Baiyer road hopeful of putting my Nikon to good use.

The site of the conflict was easy to find, for the roadside was lined with the vehicles of whites who, like myself, had gathered in anticipation of some highly charged entertainment. It was located at a bend in the road overlooking an area of mostly tall grass bounded by forest and bamboo thickets. There appeared to be almost as many spectators as participants.

As I alighted from my pickup on the first day, I was greeted by a white policeman with salt and pepper hair, strutting up and down trying to look important with his automatic rifle. 'Get back in your car,' he shouted.

'What?'

'You might be killed.' It was clear from the crowds that no one else had taken a blind bit of notice. There appeared to be little substance to his warning anyhow, and I suspected his presence was merely show, or to ensure the two rival groups observed the correct rules of engagement, rather than any concession to the safety of the onlookers.

Because the road occupied higher ground it provided an excellent vantage point from which to observe the action. Groups from both tribes could be seen massing about possibly 200 yards distance apart. They were dancing about waving their weapons in the air, hectoring each other, twirling around showing their buttocks and making other abusive gestures. This was clearly a case of 'sabre-rattling', as each side tried to goad the other into making the first move. The odd arrow was released without much conviction.

Limited cover was provided by the swathes of grass, and in the thickets growing along the flanks. Both sides were easily visible from our hilltop. Once again the dress code was a touch Bohemian, with traditional or Western styles, or a combination of the two, clearly acceptable. Many of the warriors carried large fighting shields decorated with bright designs in red, white, blue and black. As they danced

Tribal fight between the
Jikka and Yamuga clans,
Western Highlands

about the battlefield they made me think of the Queen of Hearts and her soldiers in *Alice In Wonderland*.

Bowmen from the Yamuga started slinking through the grass, the Jikka seemed unaware of their foes' movements. But then scouts were sent around the flank to foil the manoeuvre. The Yamuga retreated, and so it went for some time, backwards and forwards, with no sign of either side gaining any advantage.

At first it seemed there was no enthusiasm to join battle. But then matters began to reach a head. Again creeping forward, the Yamuga tried to stay hidden in the grass. It appeared as if they were finally going to take the initiative. Sensing action at last the spectators began cheering. Incensed that their position was being betrayed, Yamuga warriors without warning swung around and began racing uphill towards us.

Seeing this the whites panicked and ran for the safety of their vehicles, engines started in readiness for a quick escape. The tribesmen failed to press home the attack, however. They soon lost interest and returned to the main business of the day. After a safe interval the audience crept cautiously back to the edge of the lookout.

I found it all rather entertaining, this comical yo-yoing of warriors and spectators. It occurred a couple more times, then the sky became black and suddenly the heavens opened. And everyone – Jikka, Yamuga, spectators and police – all went home!

The next day things looked more promising. By the time I arrived the grass had been set ablaze in places, possibly to provide a smoke screen, or maybe to denude the available cover. There were two police vehicles in attendance, and the aged white officer was still trying, and failing, to look useful with his weapon. The police seemed to have given up on the idea of preventing spectators gathering. I was distracted by their presence, when suddenly there was a lot of yelling. I turned just in time to see the Jikka charge. Arrows were criss-crossing the battlefield, as well as the occasional blackpalm lance.

Jikka warriors during a conflict with their traditional enemies, the Yamuga

Hundreds of warriors had by this time joined in the fray – bowmen, shield bearers and spearmen. As the two sides merged it became difficult to determine which was which. I thought I saw one fellow go down with an arrow in him. Soon one of the police Landcruisers drove down the slope and edged slowly through the mêlée. This was either an attempt to halt the proceedings or to referee them.

Warrior School

My hilltop perch offered a wonderful overview of the proceedings, but was too far for useful photography. It was impossible for me to frame the action adequately. I had to get in closer if I was to succeed in obtaining some dramatic images. But how was I to go about it?

I decided that if possible I had to get behind the front lines with one of the factions. When the Yamuga retreated into the surrounding bush with their wounded, I thought I glimpsed a hut. I wondered whether this was a settlement. If I could reach it I believed it might be of some help. I found the idea of moving in among the Yamuga battle lines both exciting and unnerving.

I did not think the Jikka would attack me, even if they saw me with the enemy, but I could not be sure. I had seen how inaccurate bowmen were over distance, but I had no desire to become 'collateral damage'. And if the Jikka did not target me, would the Yamuga help me? There were stories of fighting warriors parting to allow white drivers through their battle lines when conflicts spilled across the main road. This alone made me feel more optimistic than perhaps I should have done.

Arriving at about ten on the Saturday morning, I abandoned the pickup some way down the road, out of sight of the police presence. Donning a bush hat and grabbing my camera bag I slipped silently into the shadowy forest. Moving carefully, I took an approach that I hoped would keep me well clear of the battlefield until I reached where I thought the Yamuga huts were.

Moving from tree to tree I crouched low, stopping at each to look around and listen. Nothing. The understorey was a dense and dappled world of green, light and dark, with denser shadows going on black. I took advantage of this as much as was possible, carefully parting my way through the growths, paying attention to the ground, lest I

Behind the Yamuga front lines in a conflict with the Jikka tribe

stepped on something that might betray my presence. At times I was practically crawling, hoping not to come face to face with something venomous.

Insects, a lone bird, the creaking of a branch, each individual forest sound somehow seemed incredibly loud, amplified to crystal clarity, as if all my senses had become honed by fear. Hardly daring to breathe, I moved on a few more yards then slowed, sure that I had heard a noise over to my left. The battleground lay in that direction. Freezing, I crouched low, partially concealed by a thicket of fleshy growths. Perspiration was coursing down my face, the salt stinging my eyes. I thought I heard distant drumbeats, then almost laughed when I realized it was my own heart hammering in my chest. Suddenly I appreciated the folly of what I was doing.

Something was burning, the smoke permeating the trees. The drifting blue haze highlighted sunbeams angling through the canopy to strike the forest floor, dappling the leaf litter. I could now clearly hear the unmistakable noise of fighting. The sound was not too close, but then again it was not very far away either.

It then occurred that I might be mistaken for a Jikka attempting a stealth attack. It would be little consolation to me if afterwards they discovered it was a white man they had killed. With that thought I stopped. I could not go on. Glancing nervously about me I turned around, and with frequent backward glances retraced my steps out of the woods, back to the road and the safety of the waiting pickup.

Driving back to Hagen I was both annoyed and frustrated at my jitters. By the time I reached town I had calmed down sufficiently to convince myself it would have been safe to go on. I must go back I told myself. If I wanted the photographs then I simply had to. There was no other way but to be there with the action.

That evening I ate my steak pensively. Roy had been out stock car racing, beating the Aussies at their own game. He was full of himself. Over dinner I spun a tale about having been to a *sing-sing*; I purposely avoided discussing my plans for two reasons. I thought Roy might try to talk me out of it, but it was more likely that he would want to come along. Neither of these options meshed with my plans. I had finally made up my mind it was what I wanted to do, and when photographing I much prefer to work alone.

My best chance of reaching the Yamuga, I reasoned, would be during a temporary lull in hostilities, or first thing in the day, before fighting commenced. Hopefully I could then talk to their leaders, and perhaps negotiate safe passage among their ranks when they next engaged the Jikka – or something like that. I was grasping at very short straws indeed.

Arriving very early the next day I found no police or audience, and no one yet on the battleground. I decided to try and work my way around the back of the Yamuga so that at least I would be approaching from their own territory and, hopefully, not surprise them into doing something that could prove disastrous. Once again I left the vehicle some way down the road then dived into the trees.

I made it this time, and to my surprise succeeded in entering the Yamuga encampment without being intercepted. I caught a group of men off guard, obviously preparing themselves and their weapons. They looked startled at first. Unsure whether they were surprised or angered at my sudden appearance, I approached them slowly, smiling with an arm raised. '*Gud moning olgeta, wantok,*' I said tentatively. Their expression gave nothing away. They replied but continued checking their arrows and other items of warfare.

A young man was passing a shield out through the door of a hut. He froze when he saw me, then smiled and came over. I thought I was in luck. He was wearing a head-dress of black cassowary feathers and had a white stripe painted across the bridge of his nose. He asked me what I was doing there, and told me there was going to be fighting. 'It will not be safe for you to stay,' he said with what appeared to be genuine concern.

It was then that I noted the absence of women and girls, all of whom I assumed had repaired to a safer location. I told the young man I wanted to take photographs of the fight, and explained that I was aware of the danger. He gave me the same warning. While we were talking other warriors were gathering, some perhaps arriving from outlying villages. A few had yellow paint daubed on their face or body. Others were carrying 8 foot spears, and in some cases a bow and bunches of barbed arrows. I saw more warshields too.

'Would the Yamuga offer me some protection?' I asked the young warrior hopefully. I argued that I was prepared to take the risk of being near the action. The younger men appeared unconcerned at my appearance in their midst, but when they saw me one or two of the recently arrived *lapuns* came over to vociferously demand I leave.

'Go back to Hagen,' they told me in Pidgin. 'This place is forbidden.'

'I just want to take some pictures,' I argued. They told me they were unhappy with my presence, afraid I might be killed by the Jikka. And that would bring big trouble from the police, they added.

When it became obvious that I was in no hurry to leave, the younger fellow said he would try to help. He spoke with some of the elder statesmen. It was clear from their rapid-fire Melpa that they were very

The young Yamuga warrior who acted as my guardian

agitated. They were definitely unhappy, that much was obvious. The exchange continued for some time. At length my young ally came over to convey unexpected news. It would be fine. I could join them, but only for a short while.

I could hardly believe my luck. Under the ægis of the young warrior, I would have to stay close by the safety of his war shield. But his priority, he made clear, would be to protect himself and form part of any offensive by the Yamuga. I accepted this and agreed that I would retreat if told to do so. Grateful for their decision I strolled over to thank the older men, but they ignored me, too intent were they on making ready for the approaching skirmish.

There was some yelling in the distance which I guessed was the Jikka spoiling for action. Many Yamuga, 200 at a guess, had by now gathered for the showdown. About half of these had already moved off through the trees, in the direction of the enemy, soon followed by a second wave, with me and my shield bearer tagging along.

Immediately we broke clear of the trees it was obvious to me what the Jikka had tried to do. Swathes of the longest grass had been destroyed, reducing the available cover. This meant that the two forces would have to meet in the open, rather than falling back on the element of surprise in a sneak attack. This type of combat might have been bad for the Yamuga, but from my standpoint there was less risk of an unexpected projectile from an enemy concealed in the thicketed flanks.

The Yamuga were spread out in front of me in a loose formation, bowmen and spear carriers as near as possible replicating the movements of their shield bearers. The latter tend to dictate the pace of the battle. Additionally some shield men carried their own lances, while many younger warriors, some looking barely old enough to be out of school, were carrying bows and a fistful of barbed arrows.

We faced a similar line-up of the Jikka, jumping up and down yelling. They began lobbing empty Coke cans and insults at us. Conflicts among Melpa speakers are as much theatre as honest-to-goodness fighting; invective is just as likely to be exchanged as well as arrows across the front line.

I swept the area with my eyes searching for danger. Arrows began flying, mostly wild or falling short. The Yamuga answered in kind. *Pheee*oo, *pheee*oo. The occasional enemy arrow flew close overhead. I ducked instinctively though in fact they were well clear of me.

Few spears were actually thrown, presumably because they were too valuable to allow them to fall into enemy hands, and are used mainly for stabbing. Clicking away at the shutter, I tried to keep pace with the action, and in particular the positions of the Jikka. The problem was that while I held the camera to my eye I was unable to see the whole field, which of course left me vulnerable.

My shield carrier began jinxing about to avoid presenting the enemy with a stationary target, and I shadowed his every move. I risked the occasional peep around the side of the shield, and fired off a couple more shots, trying to frame the action. *Pheee*-ooo, an arrow bounced off the edge of the shield. That was close.

The battle lines ebbed and flowed, first one side pressing forward, then the other. Unfamiliar as I was with their tactics it was impossible for me to work out how the confrontation was going. I had not noticed any casualties, though some warriors from both sides came within close-combat range to try to stab the enemy with their spears.

About twenty minutes into the foray I noted three old warriors standing close together in the wings. They appeared to be watching progress. One was balding and all of them had large beards. I snapped a picture. Between them they had a handful of spears, and one was leaning on his shield, which had designs in black, red and white, with black bird plumage on its topmost edge.

Afterwards I learned that the fighting shields used by the Melpa are regarded as extensions of the individual warriors, and as such have also to be decorated. The shield has a head (the upper edge) which is normally decorated with bird plumes, often of black or brown cassowary tail feathers. When the administration officially banned tribal fighting they made a bonfire of all the traditional wooden shields. Today they are made from any material that comes to hand, including sheet steel and plywood, but are painted still with the traditional designs.

Through my camera lens, I became mesmerized by one of the Jikka spearmen. He reminded me of a young Muhammad Ali and carried two blackpalm lances. Nearby was a shield carrier, and a young boy facing me, I noticed with sudden alarm, was drawing back his bow and aiming it roughly in my direction. Before I had fully framed the thought an arrow struck the shield.

There was a reply from two Yamuga bowmen to my left. Then quick as a flash I had the camera to my eye again firing off more shots. Then another arrow zinged by.

A group of old Yamuga
warriors lean on their spears
and fight shields watching
progress of the conflict with
the Jikka

My guardian decided that for me the battle was over. As we both
retreated we tried to remain within the shelter of the shield. I clicked
off a few more frames as we backtracked. Another arrow flew overhead, then a couple more. Other Yamuga men gathered nearby were
returning fire.

My Yamuga friend hustled me back to safety among the rearguard.
Thanking them for their help, I sat for a few minutes to compose
myself, allowing my pulse to steady while listening to the distant noise
of the continuing battle, sounds that have for thousands of years
echoed through this valley.

It would be cynical to dismiss these tribal fights as mere theatrics
because of the lack of casualties. They were real enough to people like
the Yamuga. For these proud warrior-farmers the conflict was very
much a real war, with real enemies.

Presently I made my way back on slightly shaky legs through the
settlement to my vehicle and back to town. 'You're barking mad,' Roy
said when I told him where I had been. 'You'll not be satisfied until you
have an arrow wound as a souvenir to show folks back home.' Though
his comments perhaps had some merit, and I had to confess that
perhaps I was a little rash, I considered the risk had been worth it. It is
not possible to travel anywhere in PNG with idle detachment because

it is an interactive country. When at a *sing-sing* one's senses are assaulted. Trekking through the jungle one slips in the mud. When driving one eats dust and dodges flying stones – and when a tribal fight was offered on a plate I simply had to be there, among the action. My philosophy is to accept life and the opportunities it offers, the difficulties and the risks.

5 Snakes and Ladders

'How much for the snake?' I asked the boy. He was carrying a green tree python in a home-made cage, cobbled together crudely from fly screen material.

'Ten kina,' he replied.

'*Em i tumas. Three kina*,' I said. There are several large and colourful species of python and boa constrictor, and this one I especially liked. It was one of the more striking. Juveniles may be yellow or brick red, but once they reach adulthood, several moultings later, they exchange their skin for the more regular green. The specimen before me was a handsome beast, about 5 feet long, coloured a vivid emerald fading to yellow along its sides. It had a line of white diamonds the length of its back.

'*Fivepela*,' said the boy, haggling like a true salesman.

I peered into the cage. The beast flicked its forked tongue at me as if tasting its potential new owner. It looked well fed. A crowd of raffish locals had gathered around, excited, to watch me barter with the youngster.

'Four kina,' I offered finally.

'*Nogat*.'

'Four kina,' waving the notes in his face.

'*Orait*.' He relented, handing over the creature.

Peering through the cage at my acquisition, I thought of dinner. It was not that I especially wished to eat snake, just that Roy and I were becoming sick of beef, and snake beat eating Spam. The extensive grasslands of the Baiyer Valley were developing cattle country, so the town was never short of beef, and we were benefiting from a steady supply of succulent T-bone steaks courtesy of the cattle research station. And excellent eating it was too, but too much of a good thing can become monotonous.

Sharing a flat and the shopping chores with Roy, the hunting this week had fallen on my shoulders, and so I arrived home with my catch. But what does one have with snake: salad, rice or potatoes and two veg, accompanied by a nice bottle of Chardonnay? Being Pommies of course, and yours truly being a Yorkshireman, we settled on chips and a pot of tea.

Roy with our dinner, *Chondropython viridis*

So we dined on snake, which was sadly disappointing. This had little to do with the two rats found in its stomach when we opened up the snake, and which, with hindsight, we both decided would probably have been better off eating. What did affect our sensibilities was the pointlessness of having to kill such a striking creature. Moreover, the severed head winked at us for almost an hour, and flicked out its tongue as it watched itself being gutted.

Different the snake certainly was and we of course were always willing to try anything – once. I have eaten possum's balls, bush rat, fruit bat, parrot on a stick, chrysalids (nice crunchy exterior with that soft chewy centre) and the juicy white grubs that thrive in rotten logs. However, we did regret killing the python and afterwards joked that there was more meat on a bat wing. So we returned to the tedium of eating T-bones.

The one thing that soon strikes a cord with life in PNG is that nothing is mundane – anomalous perhaps, but never run-of-the-mill. There are many contradictions. One is just as likely to see a woman breast feeding a piglet, as a tribesman with a bone through his nose carrying an umbrella. In a country boasting the very latest in communications technology, Highlanders still communicate by yodelling and shouting to one another from ridge to ridge.

Here, barely 6 degrees south of the equator, the excesses of rainfall can be measured in tens of feet per annum rather than its sub-divisions. And where else might one hope to find leathery-winged foxes and tree kangaroos, or forests so wet that there are freshwater shrimps in the moss? Is it any wonder then, that in a country where grass grows to twice the height of a man, rats reach the size of domestic cats?

Gargoyles and Bats

On our gold-panning expedition, Neil Ryan had told us several years earlier, while working as a *Kiap* in the Southern Highlands, he had been despatched to investigate reports of a body seen floating in the Iaro River, one of the many feeders into the Purari. During his enquiries into a possible murder he had stumbled upon a mysterious place secreted so deep within a limestone gorge that he was the first white man to see it.

We sat captivated as Neil told us about it: a roaring river, soaring canyon, large spiders, gangly vines, graceful waterfalls, former cannibals. We could barely contain our curiosity, to see, to feel it, to hear

Suspect bridge in the Southern Highlands, Roy at the wheel

and to smell it for ourselves. We decided upon one weekend in September.

Of course the rugged nature of New Guinea's interior dictates that lines of communication invariably cross the grain of the land, with all the attendant difficulties this entails. Even so we were surprised by the eight punishing hours it took to negotiate the 80 miles of back tracks and trails between Hagen and our destination, in the land of the 'wigmen'.[1]

With no 4x4 at our disposal we always went prepared. Besides rations, drinking water, extra fuel and spare parts for our vehicle we carried lengths of chain, an axe, lamps and a crowbar. Despite our precautions, however, there were often surprises for which we were never fully prepared.

The 'road' of course was anything but level. And some 20 miles from our objective one downhill stage resembled a wooden staircase where logs had been laid across in attempts to improve traction. And a bridge thrown across one ravine consisted of two tree trunks spanning the depths at about the correct width for a vehicle. Most of the transverse planks that might have completed the structure had long since either rotted away or, more likely, been purloined by villagers. We got out and surveyed what remained of the structure.

'Could be worse,' Roy ventured.

'Yes, there might have been no bridge,' I suggested, as I tested one of the logs gingerly with a foot. It was not greasy but to drive across involved more of an act of faith than I could summon. I crossed on foot, while Roy, with my guidance, slowly inched the truck across.

At last we reached the village of Pulupare; our journey's end was near at hand. It was just a motley collection of huts, but the nearest habitation to our objective. It occupied an enviable position on an eminence overlooking the lower reaches of the Iaro gorge, beyond which the panorama took in the undulating karst[2] landscapes extending deeper into the Southern Highlands.

Distant mountains, indistinct and suggestive, offered only the vaguest clues to the wondrous lands beyond. Far to the south-west and west respectively, beyond the limits of vision were the extinct volcanic cone of Mount Bosavi and the remote and impenetrable expanse of the Great Papua Plateau. South was the former cannibal territory of the Samberigi, where women once wore necklaces of human finger bones, or pairs of smoked hands slung around their necks as amulets.

Broken terrain of the Iaro
River Gorge, near Ulupare
village, in the Southern
Highlands

We bedded down in the *Kiap* house. Dawn arrived with a shiver. Plants were spangled with dew, the insect life already tuning up for a day of vocalizing. The distant view still carried a suggestion of mystery. The phenomenon we had come to see was known to the local people as Tobio. When we announced our intention of visiting it the village people were at first unwilling to help, fearing the wrath of the *masalai* (spirits). We pointed out that we had no fear of ghosts and demons, and that after all we had endured to reach Pulupare we were not about to give up at the final hurdle. Fortified by our cavalier attitude, one or two villagers finally agreed to accompany us as guides down into the gorge.

Our objective was a few miles to the north-east, reached via an ancient trading route linking the Pangia and Kagua sub-districts. To reach the site, Neil had told us, would take about an hour and a half of walking. Marinating ourselves in insect repellent, we left Pulupare initially along gently graded paths passing through scattered garden plots, and the stifling heat of *kunai* and sugar cane like a pair of Indiana Jones look-alikes.

Soon the gardens were left behind and the sinuous path became a deep trench, the red earth worn that way by the passage of time, rain and countless generations of feet. Down we went, slipping here, sliding there, the soles of our jungle boots of scant benefit along the steepening trail. Some fifteen minutes passed before the dimming forest wrapped its green cloak about us, strangling all sounds save birdcalls and the drone of insects. Here and there the path became almost like a roller-coaster descent with vines snarling our backpacks.

Further downhill we heard a strange and lazy 'woosh-woosh-woosh' through the treetops. It was the passing of a hornbill our guides told us. 'Can you hear that?' Roy asked as another sound caught his ear. I was barely able to pick out a murmur just at the threshold of perception, arising from somewhere below. We halted and listened, our conversation coming in whispers.

'Sounds like growling,' I said. The noise gradually increased until it was a bass rumble drifting up through the trees. The way had by this time grown rockier underfoot, demanding our undivided attention if we were to avoid tumbling into the scrub-obscured canyon on our right flank.

Near the bottom of the gorge the track without warning fell away, a vertical cliff barring our way. To continue we had to descend a series of flimsy sapling ladders lashed together with rattan to whatever might offer a little purchase. Though it remained invisible through the jungle cover we could sense the presence of something large and menacing. My pulse was set racing.

The sapling ladder on route into the Iaro River Gorge during the first exploration of the Tobio Cave

Rung by creaking rung we negotiated the ladders, hardly daring to look down. At last we dropped with relief to a broad limestone shelf beside the river.

'Jeeesus,' was all I could manage to say as I stood riveted by the frightful sight before me. I was looking at an enormous chasm, which at a conservative estimate I guessed was around 180 feet in height and 80 wide. Inside it was as black as a coal cellar on a moonless night. It must have been one of the largest river caves in the world.

Abandoned upper entrance
to the Iaro River Cave

We moved closer, better to wonder at the mysterious depths and imagine the caverns that must surely lie beyond the opening. The river roared, and I felt awed in the presence of such untamed power. The noise was deafening. The maw of this huge underground compartment was veiled in a mist, out of which emerged the river like a stampede of white horses. It galloped down a narrow, white-walled canyon, over-hung here with vines, there with gangling lianas, shot through with a venomous green light filtering down through the overhanging jungle. We gazed down this dangerously alluring cleft and could see great waves and stoppers rising and falling, rising and falling to a distant vanishing point.

Prior research had taught us that the Iaro has its source high on the southern catchment of Mount Giluwe, some 45 miles distant. After a devious course through rough bush country it goes eventually to ground, later resurfacing in this gorge. Some 13 miles upstream, on the bush road to Pulupare, we had crossed it and it seemed a respectable river, even in what we took to be normal flow conditions. Neil had told us how in his *Kiap* days he had been to the downstream opening of the gorge, below the cave, and seen how the Iaro was literally squirted between confining cliffs barely 10 feet apart.

'We can come back,' Roy said, 'at another time.'

'Yes,' I said, but with little real enthusiasm. Just beyond the entrance zone I saw huge tree trunks jammed, apparently, in some submerged crevice. They waved about in the current like ears of corn in a breeze: to fall in the river was unthinkable, to explore the passage impossible.

'And make a film,' Roy added.

'Maybe,' I said. 'But the river cave will still be impossible.'

'What about that high-level tunnel?' We could see the darkened recesses of another, smaller cave clearly visible some way above and to the left of the river exit. It was unexplored and inviting. The river passage would probably remain impassable, but the climb to this upper level did not appear to be too difficult. And it might just lead into an easier section of the underground canyon. If tree trunks had been washed through, we reasoned, there must be a wide open sinkhole.

'Yes, why not?' I said after some thought. 'We can try again at a later date. Maybe on another visit we could find the point where the river disappears.'

Back in Hagen our thoughts rarely strayed from Tobio and its tantalizing river. If we returned, could we safely explore the cave? We would be grasping at a very short straw, certainly.

The first weekend in October provided the earliest opportunity for a return. The wet season had begun so we fully expected a tough journey in our two-wheel drive Stout. We were not disappointed. It was ten that evening before our pickup finally coughed and lurched to a standstill in Pulupare, bearing myself, Roy and three weary and mudspattered co-adventurers. John Brooksbank had asked if he could come along, as had two other VSOs, Brian Heathcote and John McCarie.

'Does this truck have a clutch?' Ian quizzed Roy.

'Why?'

'Well, I haven't seen you use it yet.'

The roads were indeed so bad that conventional driving techniques counted for little. At one point, if it had not been for a bulldozer, conveniently parked nearby, we would probably still have been bogged to the axles.

Roy and 'Silkworm' John
surveying the damage on
the drive to Ulupare

It was clear our VSO friends had precious little idea what they had let themselves in for. Roy and I had several years' experience of adventure and pioneering, both underground and on the surface, in some of the world's wild places. But our companions knew little of genuine exploration.

The air was already muggy and buzzing when we stirred at seven the next day. Marshalling our equipment, Roy made final checks to ensure that everything still worked after the journey, while the remainder of us organized carriers to help porter the loads down to the cave.

It was almost three hours before we were at last mustered by the river entrance and the real task of exploration could begin. There had been a few worrying moments. At one point with our hearts in our mouths, we had looked on as one of the porters took it on himself to climb down the sapling ladders with the trunk containing our delicate camera equipment balanced across his shoulders. One slip would have dashed Roy's hopes of movie-making.

After once again marvelling at the river, we focused our attention on the upper levels. The rock climb did indeed prove simplicity itself. We protected the route with rope to a broad shelf some 20 feet above, afterwards hauling up the equipment. The ledge, we found, was roomy enough to park a couple of buses. From this point a passage of railway tunnel proportions floored with dried mud swept around to our right. Eagerly following this, we traced it for no more than 200 feet, before being brought up short, on an exposed perch overlooking the angry river at least 80 feet below.

Back at the head of the climb, a short scramble led us to the entrance we had seen from below. Keyhole shaped, it was 6 feet wide and 15–20 feet in height. Being the first to enter a cave is a bit like being an Egyptologist opening a pharaoh's tomb for the first time, and wondering what treasures awaited within. And with as much anticipation we silently filed one by one into the ancient gallery. A cool breeze wafted out of the darkened recess to fan our faces in the most alluring manner.

With the thundering river behind us our ears gradually grew accustomed to the silence. The only sound was water dripping into a hidden pool. The gallery was suffused by a dank smell, as of a disused cellar, or indeed a cavern that was ancient when the Egyptians were young. Our lamps stabbed optimistically at the million-year night, as out of the sepulchral gloom emerged nature's own fantastic creations.

'LOOK at this … look at this,' someone's shout echoed, his beam lancing through the profound darkness, washing across ghostly stone 'chandeliers', and painting wavering shadows among calcite columns, stalactites and strange twisted forms. I was spellbound by the beauty of the scene before us – a petrified forest, unyielding like its counterpart hundreds of feet above, but in this case white rather than green, crystal rather than living wood, and lacking the loathsome leeches and ravenous insect life.

Stalagmite bosses, some linked to the ceiling of white calcite tracery to form Greek colonnades, vied for attention with alabaster dripstones, and 'cascades' frozen in mid-leap. Intricate protruding forms there were, twisted into a multitude of shapes. From above, many gangly growths hung suspended among groups of stalagmites resembling plump dwarves in white, pointed hats, marching to work through a fairytale wood of 'candy' trees.

Words, I thought, fail explorers when faced with such marvellous works of nature. But, one might ask, why try to capture them with words? Is it not enough simply to be present, and become absorbed into – and content with – nature's secret creations? Who could wish for more?

I was jarred out of my reverie by another excited call from some distant alcove of the cavern. I looked around me, boulders everywhere. They littered the floor, having lost their fight with gravity, to tumble aeons ago from roof and walls and to rest where I now found them, jammed together in jumbled confusion: rocks of all sizes, some the size of cars stacked at the angle of rest like wrecks in a scrapyard. The route through them was fraught; a mere shout possibly the trigger that would precipitate them into the unknown with dire consequences.

We negotiated climbs, scrambling gingerly over obstacles. The boulder floor reared steeply ahead. The crest of the pile, we found, merged seamlessly with the floor of a more spacious hall, a chamber with a high, vaulted ceiling. As I searched around the walls for a way on I was quietly talking to myself, and was startled to hear my words repeated, like whispers in a crypt, flung back in my face by walls only vaguely sensed in the gloom.

Suddenly we became aware of the bats – lots of them. Not on the roof but on the wing, an urgent nose-to-tail mass of them flying to and fro, obviously through a passage of which only they knew. Everyone began searching for this secret flightpath, cautiously tiptoeing around the chamber inspecting the bases of the walls, poking about here, there, in the boulders of the unstable floor. And then we found it, an obscure hole leading down, hidden behind an enormous boulder.

While Roy began filming with the VSOs I investigated the continuation of this subterranean basement. It was reduced to just 4 feet high, and with the frantic traffic in bats, the way forward became a trifle busy. Following the winged bats at length led me into a lofty rift passage extending at right angles to my point of entry. It was sufficiently wide for six people to walk abreast. Grotesque stalactite forms hung from the roof, gnarled and knobbly like fat-faced baroque gargoyles. In the distance I could see a soft green hue.

Returning to my companions, I conveyed the news and together we explored, filming as we went. The high rift cut straight through the rock for several hundred feet more, to where a narrow canyon revealed itself as the source of the light. We emerged into a sudden flush of warm air. Squinting against the brighter light of day, we saw that the sheer walls rose vertically some way above us, decorated with a host of tropical extravaganzas.

Setting off down the canyon we passed a waterfall as delicate as a bridal veil, cascading like fine lace down the limestone walls into a cool, inviting font fringed with outsized ferns. Many other openings beckoned from the soaring cliffs, but a lack of time dictated that we peer into just one, where we found a fearful-looking spider covered in

The Iaro River Cave (known locally as Tobio) first explored by the author, Roy Blackham and friends. Roy (waving) can be seen in blue shorts at the bottom centre of picture

A large bush spider, a frequent encounter in the forests

fur! The creature was just sitting there, its eyes glaring coldly, as if guarding the sanctity of the cavern's innermost recesses.

Striding over the palm-sized arachnid we continued along the silent gallery, which as it happened after only a few more yards closed down where a narrow fissure barred further progress. We turned around and made our way out. My *bête noir* had vanished. With no desire to linger, we exchanged the cool of the underground for the humid warmth of the continuing canyon, at length reaching the base of the original climb up to the high-level galleries.

Daylight Robbery

A reception committee was there to greet us in the shape of a large party of excited tribesmen. We were a little nonplussed by this attention. Were they here to congratulate us on having survived the inner realms of the subterranean spirits? No. Their ranting made it patently obvious they were not a newly formed fan club.

'*Olsem wanem?*' I shouted to one of the men who had acted as porter. He told us that the other people said the cave was forbidden.

We should never have entered it.

'But we already have,' Roy said. 'Tell them we are sorry and will not do it again.' But unbeknown to us the cave passed beneath the tribal lands of this second clan. We had paid the Pulupare people to porter our gear to the cave, but this truculent group believed the income was rightfully theirs. We tried to reason with them.

'*Dispela hul bilong ston i tambu,*' they yelled, waving their arms. '*Tambu tru.*' They told us again we should not have entered the cave. It was their territory above it. '*Nau yupela mas baim long taim yupela kissim dispela hul. Kina bilong mipela.*' It was clear they wanted paying for the privilege of having entered the cave.

'No way!' I said defiantly.

'*Yupela paim mipela planty kina.*' This from an agitated man who was clearly their spokesman.

'*Nogat tru.*' We started packing our gear, trying to ignore the chief protagonist. The two tribes continued arguing, bellowing at each other, wildly gesticulating. Then they began ramping up the heat.

'*Planty kinas,*' they yelled at the Pulupare villagers. And pointing in our direction. '*Planty kinas.*'

'I don't like the look of this,' Ian said.

'Forget them,' I spat.

'We've paid the porters,' Brian added. 'We're not giving them money as well.' We made a move towards the lowest of the sapling ladders, only to find that it, and the one above it, had been torn down, effectively preventing our return up the lower walls of the canyon.

The argument was becoming more and more heated. Roy was pouring on the charm but seemed to be getting nowhere with the bellicose tribesmen. They were going over and over it time again, the fact that we had violated a *tambu*, that they wanted paying. And we just dug in and reiterated that we were not paying a penny.

One fellow strode across and, with increasing rancour, once again demanded that we give them money. Then the argument became physical. The two tribes turned their attention from us and started fighting, thankfully without weapons, just fists. We looked on with growing apprehension. They continued to demand payment. Seeing no other way out, we handed over what money we had between us.

There was a crashing noise as two men, locked in a bear-hug, wrestled themselves over a drop and plunged noisily into the undergrowth. One of the Pulupare men started yodelling up the gorge, presumably to their kinsmen in the village 1,500 feet higher. To make matters worse rain started falling, not heavy but with a persistent drizzle that soaked us anyway. Our captors were demanding more money. And Roy was still attempting to win them over. I was showing one tribesman the linings of my pockets to show that I had no more money. Brian suggested that we start rebuilding the ladders while Ian, who had by far the best Pidgin skills, continued to try to placate the two factions, who were still earnestly laying into one another.

As we hurried to rebuild the ladders I could clearly hear the sounds of fists connecting with flesh. I was wondering how we would get out of this unscathed. There was a great deal of shouting and crashing about in the brush.

We managed to patch together the ladders sufficiently to make our escape. We fully expected the warriors to be on our tail once they realized we were gone. The lights and heavy batteries we abandoned but we had the camera and, importantly, all the film plus our personal belongings.

And, as we hung on for sweet life from the swaying wreckage of the ladders I thought how glad I was they were not armed. The sounds of fighting thankfully faded the higher we struggled up the slippery path. 'I've never seen a Yorkshireman empty his pockets so fast,' Roy chuckled between gasps.

'Bastards,' I managed to hiss between breaths.

'Spoken like a true Tyke,' said John.

The rain began falling with more determination. We were wet through, water dripping off our hats and running down our noses and necks. We had precious little control over our upward progress – three tentative steps forward, slithering two back again.

Part of the way up we met a dozen or so Pulupare men, reinforcements armed with axes, bows and bunches of arrows, pounding helter-skelter down the trail towards us. Without a word of recognition they swept on by, shouting, and had soon disappeared out of sight around a bend. As they passed we marvelled at the way their bare feet gained traction in the wet clay of the path, their toes visibly gripping the ground in complete contrast to our own pathetic locomotion. We could hear faint discordant shouts from way below and I wondered what we had started.

And so it was with some measure of relief that finally we flopped over the top of the gorge and with some urgency walked the remaining distance back to the village. Our pick-up was still where we had left it.

And still there was no one following us. Not wishing to push our luck further than we had already, we hurriedly threw our belongings into the back of the vehicle, piled in after them and, with the urge to put some serious distance between us and the Tobio cave, bade a thankful farewell to Pulupare.

Suddenly the massed warriors moved in for the *coup de grâce*. All around us locals jeered and whooped, and began hurling missiles at the screen: soda cans, bottles, whatever came to hand. Then the police moved in to quell the disturbance. This was the unexpected climax, a couple of weeks after returning from Tobio, of a visit to the 'haus flea' to see the film *Zulu*.

Hagen town might lack some of the modern contrivances the developed world takes for granted, including television, but, I thought, who needs soap operas when entertainment of this calibre is available for 2.50 kina?

Unlike Africa and the Americas, PNG came out of its colonial past with relatively little bloodshed, and thanks to its German, British and Australian administrators over that period, mostly with dignity and aplomb. This was due in no short measure to the Australian programme, from the 1960s onwards, of fast-tracking the embryo nation towards self-determination. Cash-cropping and the development of natural resources were an integral and important part of this process.

During the late 1970s and well into the 1980s the newly independent state actively pursued a policy of 'nationalization', which meant that any positions, initially in the public sector but later including all jobs, held by expatriates were systematically replaced by PNG nationals. I myself was later employed by the Civil Service Commission for the Plant and Transport Authority, and with nationalization I had to be shadowed by a New Guinean counterpart. I found it increasingly difficult to take the process seriously. I shared an office with my *alter ego* who, as in most cases, was barely qualified to take over the job when I finally left. He had to countersign any document I signed. If I made a decision he had to concur, if I perspired so did he.

There were other aspects about life in PNG that I struggled to take seriously. How, for example, could one take seriously a police force that dressed like boy scouts? I soon learned, for one balmy evening I was pulled over by a police car. When the officer told me that one of the headlights on my vehicle was defective, I pointed out that one of his brake lamps was also out. At that point he pulled out his gun. 'Don't make life difficult for me, white shit,' he said, rather crassly.

Did he call me white shit? I thought as I stared down the barrel of his revolver. I could take the racial slur, but the hairs on the back of my neck were standing to attention as I rapidly learned respect for the finger attached to the trigger. 'Yes sir,' I said.

Another, more amusing, event occurred when tribesmen arrived at the Autoport to buy new Toyotas. It was clear that they had been collecting money over months, years perhaps, in villages for miles around. The 'big-men' would arrive in the morning intending to pay the asking price entirely with low denomination coins hauled in by the sacks-full. Counting would take all day and invariably drive Brian, the manager, scatty. He absolutely hated it and once or twice tried coercing either Roy or me into helping.

We avoided this at all costs, claiming we were engineers employed to fix trucks, and not bean counters. This only made Brian seethe even more. Counting the money was not made any easier by the fact that the coins often had to be sorted, since besides the legal tender, kinas, the hoard would also include Australian dollars and German marks, throw-backs from earlier colonial phases.

6 Flight of the Locusts

They appeared from the undergrowth, hideous to behold, two dozen figures, moving in a slow zombie motion, like the measured movements of T'ai Chi. With skin a greyish-blue, their nightmarish heads were bloated with mouths forming hideous grins full of broken teeth. Snake skins decorated the heads, some had noses pierced with bamboo, or the curving white tusks of wild boar. Others had bulbous craniums cracking like crazy paving.

A Mud Man from the Matt Tribe of the Asaro Valley

These non-men – demons of the forest – sent all who cast eyes upon their ghoulish countenance hurrying before them in fear. They were the famed Mud Men. Roy and I had arrived at Chuave in the eastern Simbu, about 80 miles south-east of Hagen, to witness a grand National Day gathering of cultures and clans. Wearing their best make-up and plumes and bearing arms, many tribes had trekked from

A Nambaiyufa family group smoking bamboo pipes, Simbu Province

miles around to participate in the *Sing-sing bilong Niugini*. Countless groups were there, but it was the outlandish Mud Men who stole the show.

The Matt tribe, as they are really known, inhabit the Asaro Valley east of the Daulo Pass, and number just a few hundred individuals, one of the smallest tribes in the country. Their masks, fashioned from the glutinous mud found in the Asaro, are the central prop of their strange ritual. According to current tradition, having been pursued by their foes into the muddy Asaro, they emerged slowly from the depths like spirits returned, mud-covered and hideous to behold. The sight of them put their enemies to flight and the Matt warriors won the day.

The Chuave festival proved an awesome spectacle of histrionics in which tribes danced in their finest feathers, and competed with one another in a tradition that began with the first Mount Hagen Show in 1964. The latter was held at the behest of the Australian colonial authorities in order to bring together, in a day of peace, the thousands of disparate tribal groups, many of them traditional foes.

Mud Men aside, two of the strangest sights that day were the Moss Man, swathed like the Celtic 'Green Man' of English forest folklore, and the small group that preferred to while away the day with fire licking from clay pots moulded to their heads. '*Apinun*,' I greeted the Moss Man, enquiring if it was all right to take his photograph.

'Two kina,' he demanded.

We agreed on a fee and as I framed my pictures it suddenly occurred to me that I had no change with which to pay him. Asking if 'he' could split a 10 kina note, to my amusement he pulled from beneath his sartorial vegetation a handbag, in which he rooted around a minute or two before handing me my change. Not for the first time I thought, what wonderfully amazing people.

A so-called Moss Man at the Chuave celebrations

At the end of a fascinating day, rather than returning directly to Mount Hagen, we opted for a teeth-jarring circuit around the dramatic wedge of Mount Elimbari. We dallied to admire the Nambaiyufa Amphitheatre, and marvel at the array of ancient rock paintings (mostly lozenge motifs and hand prints) and petroglyphs adorning a limestone cliff.

Being such a rugged nation, PNG is a mountain lover's paradise. The Wahgi Valley, for instance, is flanked by some of the country's highest summits: Sigul Mugal, Angalimp, Kabangana. I had been drawn to these lofty peaks for some time, and this was again the case the day we drove to Chuave.

Rock art at the Nambaiyufa
Amphitheatre, Simbu
Province

The thought of climbing some of these heights haunted me, and just occasionally while bouncing along the valley road a summit in the vicinity of Kundiawa had been dusted white, as though someone had tossed a dust sheet over it. This was Mount Wilhelm, which at just under 15,000 feet was the highest point in the country.[1] It was an intriguing sight, as I never knew for certain whether what I saw was a light sprinkling of equatorial snow, or merely a heavy frost. But I was determined that one day, whatever it took, I would stand on that peak.

Quite unexpectedly that day arrived when Neil Ryan casually enquired whether Roy and I might be interested in climbing Wilhelm. Of course we eagerly accepted.

Talair, the third-level airline operator that handled most of the short hop domestic flights, proved a boon. Through his connections with the company Neil was able to work a few 'beneath the counter' strings. Using a long weekend for the ascent, Neil told me, we could save time by flying into Keglsugle, a hamlet boasting the highest airstrip in the country. I supported his plan for two reasons. First it would spare us the treacherous road journey through the Simbu Gorge; and secondly at 8,400 feet Keglsugle would form an excellent springboard from which to climb the nation's highest peak. On the downside, flying in would deny us the chance to acclimatize.

Our proposed climb bore some similarities to that of Mount Hagen – identical cloud forest with the same mosses and vine bamboo, *pandans* and cycads. Where it differed was in the longer approach, its two bodies of fresh water, a significantly rockier landscape beyond the tree line, and of course its greater height.

We decided not to employ any carriers or guides. Our wilderness experience ensured that we were capable of making the right judgement calls if the weather deteriorated, in the event of an emergency.

On the appointed date Roy was indisposed so just Neil and I set off. Our aircraft was a twin-engined Cessna 402, and Bill, the pilot, was an ex-RAAF Vietnam veteran as many of the bush pilots were. His ability was confirmed the moment we put down on the tiny airfield. The dirt strip had been hewn from a jungle-covered mountainside and was skewed at an angle, with a shear drop-off at the approach end. Pilots

The upper of the two lakes encountered at over 11,000 feet on Mount Wilhelm

had no choice but to land uphill: the consequences of being caught in a strong downdraught at the final moment of approach was not a prospect to be relished.[2]

The Roof of New Guinea

Just before ten in the morning Neil and I said goodbye to Bill, agreeing to meet him back in Keglsugle in three days' time. Hefting our backpacks we headed out into the bush. There then followed a long day of laboured climbing, picking our way through moss forest. At around 10,000 feet we emerged into a sub-alpine grassy valley with a classic U-section – evidence that it was formed during the last Pleistocene glaciations, some 10,000 years ago. The interface between the grasslands and the forest apparently marked the snowline from this period.

It was a stark contrast stepping from the cool forests into the fierce tropical sun. For three hours we suffered beneath a cloud-free cobalt sky, threading our way through what I came to regard as porcupine grass (similar to the spinnifex of Australia) because of the hardened tips. These were so sharp that after an hour our unprotected lower legs were pock-marked with countless wounds. It was a relief, then, when we reached the mountain tarns some 2,000 feet above the tree line and pitched camp for the night.

The sun set early, so there was little to do after our meagre dinner except lick our wounds and turn in to try and secure a

The author's camp at 11,830 feet on Mount Wilhelm

decent night's sleep before making our bid for the summit, still almost 3,000 feet above. Rest rarely comes easy at altitude, and I slept uneasily. My fitful night was additionally disturbed by something scratching around the tent. I could distinctly make out some creature moving around the tent. In the still of night it sounded huge.

'Neil. You awake?' I said, digging him in the ribs.

'I wasn't,' he groaned. 'What time is it?'

'Dunno. There's something outside. I can hear it snuffling.'

'Go on, have a look then,' he said, rolling over.

'You go,' I replied, sharply. In the end I peered through the zip door. Nothing. The sky resembled a sheet of velvet set with trillions of twinkling gems.

Next morning was glorious. We surfaced to a chill air with the cut-crystal clarity that follows torrential rain. There was no signs of whatever had been prowling around the night before, not even footprints.

The views were extensive. There were lens-shaped cloud formations below us bending over some prominent buttresses. Through the thinning vapours we enjoyed a glimpse of the world below. Another shift of the cloud and the prospect vanished.

After a hurried breakfast we zipped up the tent and departed for the top. Clouds were already courting the crags high above. The giddying route skirted the edge of scarps overshadowing the upper lake. While the going was not too tough it was slow, owing to the altitude. And one had to pay constant attention to the ground ahead. One moment it was grassy, the next rocky underfoot, at other times just a few vague scratches in a rock-strewn moraine overhung by beetling cliffs.

The higher we climbed the more difficult the way became, our laboured breathing coming in rasps. Clouds swirled around us like damp rags and then parted, allowing fleeting views of angular bluffs, grey-streaked going on black, looming over us. We picked our way ever upwards through granite boulders and broken rocks of all sizes, with pieces skittering and dancing down-slope, dislodged by our faltering steps.

A lazy wind with a hint of solid rain rattled our anoraks and scythed through us, despite our protective clothing. Grey pennants of mist whipped by, and for a moment I thought I heard voices, but then the noise, whatever I had imagined, was snatched away in an instant.

After an hour a rocky niche offered some respite from the elements. We took advantage of this to partake in a little high energy sustenance before continuing. Neil announced he was not feeling too good, but when I suggested that perhaps we should turn back he refused. Apart from the chill and a shortage of breath I was feeling just fine.

After ten minutes we resumed the climb, slowly. The trail threaded its way alternately through scree and among rock outcrops that loomed up suddenly out of the gloom. Once again I thought I heard voices. Neil was some way behind me, and I could just hear him sucking at the air. Halting for a breather, I squinted down-slope and saw my companion's halting form, ghost-like, a fleeting vision one moment and gone the next, hidden by the swirling cloud.

The occasional clatter of a stone marked our continued, albeit agonizingly slow, progress. There was a louder crash below and I heard rocks bounding and thudding unseen into hidden depths, the noise gradually fading into barely discernible rattles and chattering.

'Neil! Are you OK?' I shouted into the mist.

'Yeah,' came the faint reply. When he again caught up I thought he looked pale and drawn.

At about 14,000 feet the way levelled out for a while. Neil was doubled over, retching repeatedly. Fearing the onset of hypoxia, I thought again that we should really abort the climb, but he vetoed the idea; we were so close to the top now. He was sick for about five minutes more, then we carried on. A light rain by this time had turned to hail which, driven before the wind, was gathering in fissures and cracks, piling up behind stones and collecting in the pockets of our waterproofs.

Traversing around several rock-strewn gullies we climbed a rib and suddenly found ourselves on a ridge, with no clear idea of where we were, or even whether we were heading towards or away from the summit. A fortuitous break in the weather momentarily revealed the summit plinth, and we enjoyed our first (and only) clear view of the way to the top. We committed the vision to memory before it was stolen from us for ever, then set off, inching nearer our goal.

The way ahead seemed to become more pronounced and easier to follow, tracing a line along the northern side of the arête. After about half a mile we saw ahead of us the steep final climb to the summit pyramid. Scrambling became the order of the day. Though it remained invisible we could sense a great void to our left, and we knew that the Ramu (north) side of Wilhelm fell away indeterminate. At last, tired

and wheezing, we hauled ourselves up the last few ledges to stand on the very apex of PNG's rock-girt roof.

The view south from the lakes camp at 11,300 feet on Mount Wilhelm

Of course the lack of a view was to be expected, but it was no consolation to know that it is possible to see both coasts, and around all the cardinal points a horizon pricked by countless summits.

Three hours later we were back at camp recovering in our sleeping bags. I was pleased with myself. Neil seemed to be suffering no ill effects from his ordeal, and although the climb had been tougher than Mount Hagen I had suffered nothing worse than the effects of the dreaded porcupine grass.

We strolled into Keglsugle the next morning, with time in hand before the flight out. Take off was enlightening. The technique was to run downhill, drop off the end of the airstrip, then hopefully gain sufficient height to clear the forested hills immediately ahead.

I had not really grasped how short the airfield was when we had landed three days earlier, but now as we bounced and bumped along, it rapidly become shorter. We had almost reached the end and still the

ROY BLACKHAM

Sunset on a Papua New
Guinea beach

wheels had not left the ground. My eyes were boring into the back of
Bill's head, willing him to pull back on the stick. Out of the side
window I noticed a tribesman leaning on a spade. All at once we ran
out of runway.

We dropped several feet, and my stomach lurched. Then we began
gaining height, but too slowly, I thought. Ahead I could see the wooded
ridges looming closer as we banked to starboard, still climbing.
Eventually we cleared the trees – just – and Bill lined up our course
with the sinuous defile of the Simbu Gorge.

The Festive Season

As the year's end approached, I took stock of my situation. Despite the
work at the Autoport, there were compensations. Hagen had a thriv-
ing party circuit, there was the 'haus flea', Roy had his stock-car

racing, I played squash, and of course there was the bar at the Hagen Park Motel. And there was the anticipation of our intended participation in the British expedition.

In December a few VSOs began to hanker for the coast and a festive season with a difference – scorching sand rather than snow, surfboards instead of sledges. Roy and I decided to go with Ian McCarie and 'Silkworm' John for a week in Wewak. Accompanying us were Cedric Tuffy, a civil engineer with the Plant and Transport (PTA) Department, and a girl called Liz Taylor.

Wewak, I was delighted to find, was an idyllic little north coast town partially straddling a small headland. It was sandwiched between a belt of mangrove swamps and miles of unspoiled sandy beaches fringed with listing coconut trees. Liz provided the accommodation. Her house was overhung by palms, and softly cocooned in an overgrown garden of hibiscus, frangipani, jasmine and bougainvillaea. After dusk, the sweet-scented air was a very welcome balm after the ubiquitous dust and grime and roughneck life of the Central Highlands.

Most of our indolent week in Wewak was spent on the dark sand beaches, enjoying the surf. We partook of iced drinks at the Windjammer Hotel, a watering hole situated a few convenient strides from the water's edge. It was the ultimate lazy holiday, all Bali Hai.

Halfway through our time on the coast I travelled out to Cape Wom, some 7 miles west of town, and was surprised to come upon a pyramid-like war memorial, a disused airfield and an anti-aircraft gun. The north coast apparently saw some of the heaviest fighting of the Coral Sea campaign of the Second World War, and a plaque announced that on 13 September 1945 it was here one Major-General Robertson accepted the Japanese surrender.

It is perhaps a little known fact that over 30,000 New Guineans were conscripted during the war. They became known as the 'Fuzzy Wuzzy Angels', and they worked mostly as porters but 2,000 of them died from illness or wounds. Thousands more entered military service in the Papuan and New Guinea Infantry, and fought jungle campaigns.

Back in Hagen we saw in the New Year at Cedric's bachelor pad to the tune of Tchaikovsky's '1812 Overture' played at full volume in glorious surround sound. Outside someone was celebrating by rolling and banging bins in the street. Wewak had already become a dust-clouded memory. It had been quite a year, the new one promised to be even greater.

Unfortunately the New Year started on a bad note. I was returning from the Simbu and a quest for dramatic photographs, when I drove around a bend to find the main highway ahead of me strewn with bodies, some with limbs at unnatural angles. A mixed group, I saw, were crouched at the roadside wrapped in filthy *lap-lap*. There was a deep scrawl mark in the road but no sign of any vehicle.

I slowed, and in the same instant I had an instant flash-back to the Baiyer River incident. The road dropped away to the left, the direction in which I assumed the missing vehicle had gone, while to my right a high, wooded bank overlooking the road formed an ideal place to spring an ambush. An eye for an eye I thought once again as my mind began working overtime.

It took every ounce of willpower to override my natural instincts. I wanted to stop, but with my earlier scare still quite vivid, instead I simply slowed down and began weaving through the bodies littering the road. There was a bump from the rear and I dearly hoped it was a stone I had run over. I cleared the last of the bodies, then with an anxious glance in the rear view mirror accelerated away in a cloud of dust. Only when I thought there was enough distance between me and the accident – 4 or 5 miles – did I stop.

The vehicle came slewing to a standstill. I slumped in the seat, shaking like a leaf. I could not help thinking about those poor people. What else was I to do? We were advised by officialdom not to stop at accidents. I had heard similar incidents where a villager had been killed and the driver had failed to stop. The *wantoks* of the deceased had merely lain in waiting to ambush the first innocent driver to come along. An eye for an eye. Payback justice in action.

I restarted the car and moved off, convincing myself that I had had another close shave. I glanced in the rear-view mirror. The road behind was clear. I drove on through Kundiawa and pretty soon was heading back into the Western Highlands, the Wahgi Valley telescoping out before me. Only then did I completely calm down.

The Coconut Express

The introduction of coffee and tea production to PNG meant that many villagers became wealthy beyond their wildest dreams. To keep pace with a growing demand for rugged vehicles a couple of dealerships had established trading outposts in Hagen. One day Roy investigated a rumour that one of these, Ela Motors, paid people to fly to the east coast port of Lae and drive new vehicles back to town. It was true! But I was amazed that they trusted strangers in this way, and also wondered what state the vehicles would be in after over 300 miles of the Highlands Highway.

We could not pass up the opportunity to be flown free to the coast, provided with accommodation and meals, plus a pocketful of money.

Quick to spot a way of making a quick killing, Roy suggested that we could load up with coconuts, which do not grow in the Highlands, for the return journey, and sell them on at a profit back in Hagen. I took a little convincing. The main trunk road from the coast into the highlands would be like participating in the Paris to Dakar Rally. Could we expect the coconuts to survive such a journey? Would we? But I finally agreed and we headed for Lae.

Diving steeply to Kundiawa during our unscheduled landing

My Wilhelm climb was still fresh in my memory, and so during the flight east I maintained a weather eye hoping to point out to Roy the spot where I had stood. Unfortunately heavy cloud hid the range from view, but as we neared Kundiawa the pilot, without any warning, began diving towards the tiny airstrip. The unscheduled stop was a consequence of a riotous evening the night before that now had left the pilot, who had a greenish pallor, with a desperate need to land.

Keith van de Linde was Ela Motors agent at Lae, overseeing the importing and shipping of new vehicles up to the Highlands. He met us at the airport and ran us back to his place, where he fed us well and provided overnight accommodation. Over dinner he quizzed us about our intentions for the following day. We replied casually that we might have an amble around town, buy a few things, then set off back to Hagen around lunchtime. Keith's eyes started from his head.

'Lunchtime!' he exclaimed. 'If you don't clear the Markham by then you'll never make it.'

'What's the problem?' I asked.

'The heat, that's the problem,' he said with some alarm. The Markham Valley, he told us, was about 100 miles long, virtually at sea level the whole distance, and hemmed in on both sides by towering mountains. Once beyond the littoral fringe, and what little breeze the ocean proximity afforded, it would be like being at the focus of a solar furnace.

'What's a bit of heat?' I said somewhat off-hand. 'We came here to get away from the cold.'

'Besides, the road's shit,' Keith added. 'You'll be lucky if you can manage thirty miles an hour. If you're away by seven, you still may not reach the Kassam by noon.' The Kassam Pass was the gateway to the Central Highlands. Of course we had no intention of rising early.

'We like hot,' Roy ventured. 'Besides I've been to Iran, where it's a lot warmer than here.'

'Will the vehicles be ready in the morning?' I asked.

Keith's face lit up. 'Sure, all fuelled up and ready to go.'

'OK, that's fine then,' I said.

'You're going at first light then?'

'No,' we both chorused.

He laughed nervously. 'Well, it's your funeral.'

'We may not get down this way again,' Roy explained. 'Anyway so long as we have plenty of water and don't have any problems with the pickups, everything will be fine.'

'We know what we're doing,' I said, sincerely hoping this was true. From what Keith was saying I fully expected to see a road littered with abandoned vehicles, bleached skeletons gripping the wheel, skulls a mask of agonizing death.

The next morning we collected the trucks, and said farewells. 'Don't worry. We'll be fine,' I said.

'I guess so,' Keith shrugged with resignation. We found the local market and, for a handful of kinas, bought so many coconuts they were piled high in both pickups. Whether any would survive the journey we had no idea. We had nothing with which to secure them.

By 10.30 we were trundling past the last habitations of town. At the outset the road ran parallel to the broad Markham River, with to our right the Atzera ranges rising up in ever higher tiers into clouds hiding the lofty Huon Peninsula. Ten miles beyond Lae we passed the junction with the road to Bulolo, site of the great 1930s gold rush. Ahead of us the Markham Valley stretched into a heat haze. With good speed, we both reasoned, and a slipstream blowing by the open windows we would be fine.

Roy led off with me following. After a couple of miles I was perspiring like a Sumo wrestler. As we had found in the Highlands, the best way to attenuate the washboard unevenness of the road was to floor the accelerator and go like mad. This made our passage more comfortable, but even so we were still shaken so severely that our eyes rattled in their sockets.

Dust was a constant problem. Both vehicles were raising clouds of it stretching back maybe ¼ mile, and for the person following it was extremely disagreeable. Because of this I had to keep the windows closed, which made the heat more unbearable. Even with the windows closed grime adhered to my skin, stung my eyes and set my teeth on edge. We pulled up now and then at dusty roadside shacks to swill the dirt from our palettes, or simply to buy a few dusty bananas from makeshift dusty stalls at which dusty locals sat.

Climbing back into my vehicle I tied a cloth around my face and glanced at the coconuts in the back. The pile had certainly gone down but there was nothing for it. I had no intention of slowing down and prolonging the agony of the journey. It was about 11.30 and already it was hot enough to fry eggs on the paintwork.

About halfway along the valley I decided to pull over. Up until then all I had been able to see ahead of me was a billowing pall of white murk, and a glance in the rear-view mirror revealed more of the same. It was only the sideways view that changed, with the slow procession of the Saruwaged Mountains forming the northern flank of the valley.

It suddenly occurred to me that if I was losing coconuts over the side, then Roy must be too. Being new the pickups had yet to be fitted with the mesh guards used to protect windscreens against the flying stones of unmade roads. The idea of colliding with a coconut bouncing at 60 miles an hour unannounced out of a dust cloud did not appeal. I stopped to take photographs, but at the same time to allow Roy to pull further ahead, thus reducing the hazard of driving blind into his wake.

I got out and leaned back against the wing as I took in the vista while eating a banana with a swig of warm water. The valley was dotted with a few coconut groves, plantains and isolated trees. The latter were shimmering with the heat and resembled the flat-topped acacias seen in African safari films. In the near distance was a hut or two, their thatched roofs looking as if they needed a haircut. Beyond was a hotchpotch of green hills resembling a crumpled green quilt, rising above which was a sawtooth range of mountains like fangs set in green gums.

Behind the wheel once again I started off. With Roy well in front now I could wind down the window and allow a through-draught. A few more bumpy miles later and I had a numb feeling from the neck down. I could see my arms gripping the steering wheel but they no longer seemed attached to my body. Without the dust at least I could now see to the front. Occasionally as I rounded a bend I saw a plume of dust in the distance marking Roy's progress: there was no end to the valley in sight.

Palms were flashing by, then a corrugated hut. There were more coconut palms, a few more huts. My arms were still steering the truck, but it was almost as if I was having an out-of-body experience. And then I saw something most peculiar in the distance ahead of me. There was a strange green haze. As I stared at it, mystified, it appeared to shimmer, to change shape subtly.

As it neared it took on more substance, a grainy appearance. Then it dawned on me what it was. But no sooner had I realized than it was upon me, mutating into clouds of green missiles on erratically flickering wings. It was a swarm of locusts, flying randomly this way and that, in a madly gyrating mass, emitting a sound like old newspapers being crumpled. I ducked instinctively as the creatures smashed themselves on the windscreen. Wings, heads and bodies, one moment a creation of nature, the next a yellow-green smudge, scores of them.

Switching on the wipers produced a yellowy-green smear with just a hint of wing and leg. After a sustained squirt of the washers I blinked. Just as suddenly as I had hit the swarm it had passed on by. A few miles further on I hurtled around a bend and there was the other Toyota, with Roy leaning against the door beside a rusting tin shed, which turned out to be a trade store.

I slithered in to the side kicking up stones. Roy was smiling with a can of Coke in his hand. I walked around the Stout, laughing. The front was decorated with a green gunge. 'That was a little interesting,' Roy said.

'Hmm, just a little,' I replied. His radiator grill, I saw, was also a disaster area of body parts.

View down into the Markham Valley, from the mile high Kassam Pass, gateway into the Highlands

'We shouldn't be too far off the Kassam now?' Roy said, more by way of a question than a fact. The Kassam Pass was originally constructed in the 1950s. It winds from near sea level one vertical mile out of the oppressive valley. At the top there would still be dust, but the cooler air and lower humidity would be welcome.

We negotiated the high pass without any hitch, and hurtled through the Eastern Highlands and on into the Simbu and Chuave, followed by the long Wahgi Valley and home.

That night after showering we went straight to the Hagen Park Motel and treated ourselves to the Sunday night smorgasbord: soup, every cold meat imaginable, salads, pickles and fresh fruit salad, all for two kinas. Afterwards around the central hearth, we relaxed away the aches of the coconut run with a few irascible Aussies.

A Washout on Mount Giluwe

Hagen's VSO population were holding a party, and 'Silkworm' John's house was packed. People were everywhere, sprawled on chairs and cushions, lazing about the floor, spilling into the back garden or out

Mount Giluwe seen across the rough bush country of the Southern Highlands, in the vicinity of Kagua

onto the verandah. The party continued well into the night, with free-flowing booze loosening tongues and lubricating ideas for adventures. Brian Heathcote was there, and suggested that he might climb Mount Giluwe. Did I want to come along? Still basking in the success of the Wilhelm climb this seemed a good idea, in my drunken haze, and so I readily agreed. John, too, was keen to have a bash.

Known as Kelua in the local tongue, Mount Giluwe is the second highest mountain in the country but far more shapely than either Hagen or Wilhelm. It is all that remains of an ancient shield volcano, eroded over millennia to leave the surviving lava plugs forming twin summits, the highest being 14,330 feet. It can be seen for miles around, one of the finest views being from the roadside at the Tomba Gap, from where it appears framed by *pandans*, rising above the montane rain forest.

We gathered at the mountain's north-western approaches, beside the bush road linking Tambul with Mendi. It was a dry day and the weather was fine but with a hint of something else. Accompanying us to act as porters and camp hands were four students from Hagen College. Everyone was full of enthusiasm as we marched off into the trees shouldering large packs, taking with us a three-man tent and supplies to last four days.

Like the other high mountains Giluwe is dominated by a number of distinct vegetation zones. As we broke free of the top levels of the forest we entered a long sub-alpine valley dominated by cushion plants, tussock grasses, bogs and tree ferns as well as the inevitable porcupine grass. By following this dale we hoped eventually to reach the base of the westernmost of the twin summits. Both flanks of the valley were dotted and streaked with relic patches and fingers of ancient, stunted woodland.

Some miles up the valley we set up our first camp in the three-man tent; the carriers set about making themselves comfortable in a hunting shelter located in a small copse of gnarled trees. By dusk a fine rain had begun falling across the valley in grey sheets. The 'hut' was open at one end and barely large enough for four. Repeated attempts to light a fire eventually proved so successful that the fire rapidly burned out of control. The resulting conflagration burnt away most of the thatched roof, making the shelter virtually untenantable.

The fire was only the first of the setbacks. After a troubled night we awoke to a bleak day of low cloud and steadily deteriorating weather. For most of the day we trudged on with heavy hearts, tracing the soggy valley eastwards in the vague hope of finding a way onto the upper 'alpine' plateau, and from there a route to the summit. After several

Porters cowering in a native bush shelter during an aborted ascent of Mount Giluwe

John 'Silkworm' Brooksbank
and Brian Heathcote (with
back to camera), together
with the carriers at the first
camp, during aborted
attempt to climb Mount
Giluwe

hours in mist we finally had to admit to having no clear idea of our
whereabouts, or how close we might be to the final climb. In view of
the inclement weather and our growing exhaustion it was unanimously
decided to retreat.

7 Machetes and Bad Ju-Ju

'I would like a gun licence please,' I said to the police officer behind the desk.

'Yes, and what for?' he replied with an air of suspicion.

'Shooting snakes,' I said.

'Snakes?' he blurted as if never having heard the word spoken before.

'Yes,' I said. 'You know, long and slithery. Like a lizard but with no legs.'

'I know what a snake is,' he barked.

'Sorry. So, can I have one?'

'No.'

'Why, is there a problem?' I asked. He had developed a nervous tic which was making his left eyebrow quiver. I continued to stare at him, hopefully. Waiting.

'Impossible,' he said, at length. 'We cannot allow guns for killing snakes. They are protected by law.'

'Yes, and who's going to protect me from them out in the *bikpela* bush? I'll be walking from here to Telefomin.'

'So?'

'Telefomin is in the West Sepik Province. It's a long way.'

'A long way, yes.'

'Well,' I ventured. 'It's pretty wild country out there beyond Lake Kopiago you know, there's the Strickland Gorge, and Oksapmin and, well, it's all remote and wild. There will be venomous snakes all over the place, probably.' He continued to regard me suspiciously.

'And there are Hewa nomads,' I added. Suddenly it was as if I had uttered some secret password, an open sesame to his better nature.

'Hewa. Yes. Hmm … well, maybe you better have a gun then, hadn't you?' he said, suddenly approving.

From investigating the logistics of walking to Telefomin, I was aware that intruders into the remote territory of these tetchy bushmen had occasionally been received with volleys of arrows.

It was patently obvious from his change of heart that although it was not acceptable to shoot snakes, it was fine to take pot-shots at the Hewa. He issued me my licence and I went happily off and bought myself a nice single-barrelled shotgun, and several cartons of cartridges.

I had given up my job at the Autoport, but as it happened, several factors conspired to prevent my trekking the 260 miles westwards through the Hewa lands. The main one was a series of phone calls from Kevan Wilde, who was adamant that a reconnaissance before the British expedition team I was planning to join arrived was far more important. In the end I had to agree.

An ex-policeman turned pacifist, Kevan had been in the police in Birmingham, then Tasmania and finally here in PNG, before resigning to become a geological assistant for Carpentaria Exploration. A couple of months earlier he, Roy, an Australian, Richard Knight, and I had in eight hours made the second only descent of Bibima, at 1,600 feet the deepest cave in the southern hemisphere.

I was continuing to live at the company flat I shared with Roy until Heagney discovered that we had converted it into an expedition office, and I was using it as a clearing house for supplies arriving from sponsors. For this indiscretion I was kicked out.

During one lengthy phonecall, Kevan and I had discussed priorities and the inventory of our field equipment. More than once Kevan had been emphatic about travelling light, offering advice such as drilling holes in your toothbrush, and using a flannel for a towel. So when he arrived from Goroka at the end of March, we were astounded to find that he had one rucksack devoted entirely to smoking; it contained nothing but cigars and tobacco!

It was another couple of days before we had finally procured essential supplies: black twist tobacco and blankets for the porters, food, cooking pots, machetes and the like. Most of this we obtained from the helpful Robert Cheung, who ran one of the town's Chinese emporiums.

On a Wing and a Prayer

Roy was going to see out his contract with Heagney and join the expedition later. But Kevan and I left Hagen on 4 April for a two-month assessment of the caving potential in the Hindenburg and Victor Emanuel Mountains, a mostly unexplored expanse of territory between the Strickland Gorge and the eastern Star Mountains. I was thrilled to at last be joining one of the most ambitious undertakings ever to leave the UK.

The aim was stunning in scope: a team of twenty-four would spend six months exploring 1,000 square miles of mountainous terrain and, with luck and perseverance, would discover, explore and map the deepest cave in the world, the holy grail sought by speleologists everywhere. In that region, limestone ranged between 1,900 and over 13,000 feet in altitude. Deluged by an annual mean rainfall of up to 600 inches, water was expected to be problematic in the caves.

Once we were airborne we immediately proceeded west. The pilot, Doug McGraw, flew for the Mission Aviation Fellowship (MAF) and threw the twin-engined Cessna around like a man with God on his side. Two hours later he spotted a landmark that only he recognized and dived through a hole in the partial cloud cover. Soon we were rumbling down the dirt airstrip that serves the out-station of Telefomin.

Without delay we off-loaded our cargo, then took to the air again, flying south over the Victor Emanuels towards Olsobip to get an overview of the limestone ranges, including an extensive honeycomb

Kevan Wilde leading our carrier line through the grasslands of the upper Tifalmin Valley during the British expedition reconnaissance

karst area bisected by a fault-influenced valley, and further west a remote plateau heading the Hindenburg Wall, an impressive limestone scarp as much as 3,000 feet high. The intention was to follow this with ground trips of between two and four weeks. However, the plane was too fast and before we realized it we had crossed the fault valley without a chance to investigate the terrain. Poor weather also prevented us making any useful assessment of the high plateau, but we did notice some voluminous rivers emerging from the base of the Wall.

Although the fly-past had been of limited value, we had seen enough to believe that the area was worth investigating at ground level. Three days later we hefted our loads, and with the sun at our backs headed for the Tifalmin Valley, two days' distant and apparently inhabited by a tribe of sorcerers. With us were four trusted Eliptamin carriers, two weeks' rations and 60 pound backpacks bulging with personal gear, caving equipment, ropes, my shotgun and of course Kevan's tobacco.

At each settlement on this first day on the trail we were invited to

Telefomin man with infant. Note the cassowary quills worn through pierced nostrils

partake of a traditional greeting known as the 'Telefomin handshake'. This involved linking hands by hooking the little fingers around each other, raising the arms above head height before swinging them forcefully down. The resulting loud 'crack' as the fingers parted each time left me scanning the ground expecting to find a finger there.

The villagers went naked apart from a dainty grass 'sporran' for women, and a penis sheath for men (colloquially known to whites as a 'dick-stick'), that was sometimes straight, often curly, fashioned from a hollowed vegetable gourd, held in place with string tied around the wearer's waist. Additionally the men thrust long cassowary quills through their pierced nostrils.

After seven hours wilting through stifling *kunai* (a bladed grass up to 6 feet high of the *Imperata* species) we found ourselves at last over-looking a deep gorge carrying the Sepik. By this time I was parched as a dead lizard. Further west I saw a blue haze, hinting of distant mountains. A medley of village huts straddling the far bank was our immediate destination. We traced the dizzying trail down to where, at an abrupt narrowing, a cane bridge audaciously spanned the river. Ignoring the turgid waters beneath our feet, we gingerly crossed the structure then clawed our way up the far side, and with dusk drawing in stepped onto a park-like terrace.

Urapmin was a delightful place, landscaped with flowering shrubs and consisting of perhaps a dozen dwellings inhabited by a friendly people. Interestingly the houses were raised 2 feet above the ground with a curious entrance formed from an oval hole cut through a decorative door board. This we understood to be a defence feature; an intruder attempting to gain entry would have to stoop, and would be vulnerable to counter-attack by the occupants.

A flea-ridden night was relieved by sunbeams winking through chinks in the hut walls. The porters had already left. Without delay we breakfasted and, accepting gifts of cucumber and papaya, set off on the next stage of our journey. At the edge of the village we slithered down a muddy bank beneath the eves of the forest and in minutes we had passed like shadows into a twilight world.

Our route provided trials and pleasures in equal measure – the mud, exotic birdlife, poisonous *selat* plant, insects, colourful flowers, and a sense of mystery. My pack soon developed the habit of entangling itself with any dangling obstacle, but despite the inconveniences I revelled in the variety and at times absurd fecundity of nature.

I strolled in wonder through the half-light of strange plants: giant gingers, *Ficus* and innumerable subspecies of *Nastus productus* (vine bamboo). Delicate tendrils spiralled around scabrous boles carrying with them arum-like glossy leaves in ascending tiers. And then there were the aromas – seductive orchid fragrances, an organic reek redolent of a compost heap, the herbaceous airs evoking a summer house at the foot of an English country garden.

Sometimes we would be delighted by an unexpected splash of

Lush bromeliads decorating the boles of forest trees

colour. We gazed aloft in amazement at the gorgeous bright red blooms of the leguminous Flame of the Forest cascading from the highest boughs.

Glancing around me from time to time, I saw trees, nothing but trees. And what growths! Saplings craving sunlight, palms, spiky trees, medium-sized boles and strapping mossy trunks. I let my gaze rise to the full height of buttress-rooted giants supporting the distant forest crown, and glimpsed multicoloured parakeets like itinerant jewels, flickering raucously through the leafy canopy.

And the leaves came in all sizes and every conceivable form, heart-shaped, fan-shaped, pinnate, lanceolate, palmate, in multitudinous shades of green, some in silhouette going on black. Such diversity. I was absolutely enthralled.

Everywhere I saw was a picture of orchestrated confusion, tendrils and creepers, every imaginable kind of growth crowding in on the scene. There were lawyer vines and barbed rattans locked in aerial embrace. I marvelled at woody lianas like sleepy pythons, draping their lazy loops from low-slung boughs decorated with the luxuriance of bromeliads and epiphytes like the fabled hanging gardens of Babylon.

Once we were obliged to wade up to our waists along the reedy margins of the Ilam River, then left the forest behind, our path intersecting jungly creek beds tumbling from the forested heights on our left. Reeking in perspiration and weary but cheerful, we at last staggered into the hamlet of Fasanabip, a tiny settlement sporting a small airfield and a superbly ornate *haus tamburan*.

That evening as we cooked we made further plans. 'What do you say to leaving behind the caving gear?' Kevan suggested. I had no argument with this since the weight of my backpack was already proving irksome. We also discussed Mount Aiyang, a 10,334 foot high peak forming the northwestern bastion of a range of mountains, the Bahrmans, that comprised the southern aspect of the upper Tifalmn valley. As far as we could determine it was unclimbed and certainly had never before been visited by speleologists. It is not every day one has a chance to tackle an unclimbed peak, so with this prospect in mind *and* the chance of cave discoveries, the Aiyang became our first priority.

Shortly after nightfall we heard a commotion in the nearby village. We dispatched Yaiyok, our head porter, to investigate. '*Sanguma kilim man*,' he reported on his return. He was trembling as he told us that a man had been killed by sorcery, and a lighted *bom-bom* (a grass torch) had been placed in his hand so his spirit could rise and indicate the

house of the culprit. Sure enough, as we peered out into the inky night, we could indeed see a light bobbing its ghostly way across the valley. Being a long way from their tribal lands, all four porters were visibly disturbed by this and refused to leave the hut again until daybreak.

Soon after first light we resumed our journey, and all morning long we trekked through the grass-lands comprising the upper valley. From Fasanabip we climbed steadily for an hour or more. Although the river was hidden away to our right, a distant murmur reminded us constantly of its presence.

Eventually the gradual

D'Albertis Creeper (*Mucuna novaeguineensis*), the famed Flame of the Forest, added a splash of colour to our hikes

transition into the bush provided a welcome respite from the noon heat. As afternoon wore on we were drawn deeper into the high forest beneath Aiyang. Four hours later we arrived at a remote grass hut, where we decided to camp. Our altitude by this time was a little over 7,000 feet and we thought the hut would make an ideal base from which to climb the mountain, which towered somewhere above us still but remained invisible through the forest.

As we settled in for the evening the noise of the cicadas rose to an ear-rending pitch, setting the teeth on edge. At these latitudes the transition from twilight – usually 6 o'clock – to total darkness is rapid, usually twenty minutes. It was the same each evening; countless insects announced the imminent arrival of dusk, then, just as suddenly as it began, darkness brought an abrupt end to the din and an uneasy hush fell upon the forest. The performance was as regular as clockwork.

The next day dawned cool, with an all-pervading, wraith-like mist. Soon after vacating camp the rains came. We now had to resort more and more to our bush knives, and for most of the day knew nothing other than a strange world of stunted trees bearded in dripping moss.

Looking thoroughly dejected, the porters repeatedly told us that the mountain lacked drinking water, that it was a *ples nogut*, the abode of evil spirits. As if to underline the bad *ju-ju*, one of our trail hands slipped from a log bridge and gashed his leg with his axe. We cleaned and dressed the wound as best we could, then sent him down the trail to wait at the hut for our return.

After several hours blazing a trail the summit still eluded us. Exhausted and demoralized, we descended again to camp. The injured carrier was gone, departed for the valley it seemed. We had yet to see a hint of caves and over a meagre dinner came to the conclusion that to all outward appearances the mountain was a speleological desert. A first ascent was still within our grasp, however, and after much deliberation we opted to continue. How far we had yet to go, though, was a source of much debate.

Dawn brought little change to the weather. We regained the trail head and found the trees ahead petering out, replaced by a tenacious form of birch that resisted the keenest of blade. After another hour of climbing we glimpsed a ridge. Kevan remained behind while a porter and I forged ahead. With a final push through the undergrowth we at last gained the narrow eastern arête, and after another hour following a scrub-entangled crest finally we placed a tentative foot on the summit. Cloud of course prevented any view, so that what should have been a thrill was simply a clammy anticlimax.

South to the Finim Tel

Back in Fasanabip we met Hal Bush of the Summer Institute of Linguistics, an American organization dedicated to translating the Bible into the world's minority languages. One evening he suggested that we join him for dinner, and over a nut roast related how, together with his wife and two teenage daughters, he had been in the valley for two years transcribing the New Testament into the local tongue. We had already noticed a few nearby burial caves and quizzed Hal about these.

Extra supplies were flown into Fasanabip for us, and we struck up over the Bahrman Mountains with rations to last ten days. We had been told of a clearing 10 miles south-west of the village. It was clearly visible along with some large sinkholes on an aerial photograph of the plateau. If it was large enough, we thought it would be ideal for receiving air-dropped supplies.

The route south over the mountains involved 4,000 feet of steep ascent, relieved only once when, shortly before reaching the head of the

Impressively large forest butterfly

pass, we strode out onto a rocky knoll which offered an excellent view eastwards to distant Telefomin. It was sheer heaven to be free of the suffocating forest, no matter how briefly.

Once the pass was behind us dismal swamps and impenetrable bamboo thickets became commonplace. Often sinking to thigh level or deeper, our only pleasure in this stinking miasma was the occasional colourful butterfly, or an exotic bird call – peew...*wit* – to remind us that we were travelling through a tropical paradise, even if not always obvious. On every hand *pandans* spread their spiked fronds overhead, while others falling limp from the trees added further to the noisome organic porridge through which we wallowed.

After another hour confined to the mischievous forest we broke clear of the cheerless swamp glades. We had reached the Finim Tel at last. With nightfall approaching we picked our way through a long clearing that stretched before us like a welcome mat, to the trail's end and the prospect of a meal. We both were suffering from mycosis of the feet, and Kevan from an attack of malaria.

We had a small two-man tent, but found it claustrophobic in the tropical climate. Camp therefore was invariably a rudimentary plastic sheet on which we lay, with a second one acting as a fly. We sometimes slept beneath a mosquito net. Mosquitoes were not always problematic, and on the occasions when we shunned use of a net, we would wake from slumber to answer a call of nature, and find all manner of crawling things exploring our recumbent forms.

Our first full day on the plateau was enlightening. Guided to the south-west of the camp we were shown Le Buum Tém, a 250 foot deep shaft with what appeared to be a sizeable cave at its base. It was a surprise to learn that the Wokkamin people from the Papuan lowlands once hunted flying fox here by swinging down on vines!

Owing to the lack of accurate maps we navigated entirely with aerial photographs and a compass. The technique involved one person thrashing through the undergrowth as far as possible while still remaining within earshot. 'Wokim draipela diwai,' we would shout and he would select a tree and shake it. The compass reader would then sight the instrument on it. By this means we maintained quite accurate bearings over long distances, a skill that was a constant source of wonder to Yaiyok and the other tribesmen.

Determined machete work eventually enabled us, after two days cutting on a southerly heading, to reach two black spots we had seen

The author's rudimentary camp on the Finim Tel plateau during the reconnaissance for the British caving expedition

on the photographs. These turned out to be impressive, rock-walled shafts, each an estimated 500 feet deep. Secured to a handy tree, Kevan managed to peer into one, and saw growing at its base large trees reduced to the scale of broccoli. The pits dwarfed all other holes we had so far discovered. Doubtless there were many more, but the problem we faced was that the jungle was so thick that holes came to light only if we practically stumbled into them.

After a week on the plateau we had gleaned sufficient evidence to suggest the area offered great potential. In light of this, we started work on a bothy commodious enough to house the 24-man team, with a dormitory with raised sapling beds, a dining room plus tables and benches, a kitchen with a store room complete with shelves, a toilet block and showers. And apart from a polythene roof, all was constructed from bush materials with not a single nail.

One evening I was relaxing around the camp fire with the porters, when suddenly there was a yell. '*Oww! Mekim wanem?*' Kevan, who had been answering a call of nature, was crouched just beyond the feeble light cast by the dying fire. However, thinking the pallid apparition was a bush demon, one of the camp hands had deftly hurled a faggot into the shadows, hitting Kevan on the head! The incident definitely raised my spirits and doubtless frightened away any genuine ones.

Head porter Yaiyok building
a bridge over a jungle creek
on the Finim Tel Plateau

After almost two weeks on the plateau, with the bothy construction well advanced, a return to base became necessary. Other interesting areas beckoned and supplies were rapidly dwindling. We returned through the unpleasant swamps and over the next few days trekked back to Telefomin. After some quality rest time and a deep clean, we were off again, this time for the fault valley we had seen briefly from the air.

Crossing the infant Sepik by a vine suspension bridge, we trekked on south to the crest of a ridge, and saw another mountain range, the Victor Emanuel Mountains, ahead of us climbing to even greater heights, jungle stretching endlessly in every direction. Descending into the remote Nong Valley, we set up a simple camp within a meander loop of the Ok Anaram, the very epitome of a clear-running tropical creek.

The following day our climb resumed, taking the trading route to Olsobip, a village located on the Ok Fenang on the Papua side of the mountains. Two hours out from the Nong our route intersected a steeply inclined clearing known as Un Tém Tigiín, pierced on its east side by a deep shaft. Curious, I hurled in a handy rock, and jumped back in alarm as a 'KABooom' reverberated from the depths. The noise we guessed was consistent with a hole at least 300 feet deep, but for the moment at least, exploration would have to await the arrival of suitable equipment and more manpower.

East by Mogondabip

Leaving the great shaft we continued our upward progress, passing a rock shelter known as Borem Imal. Our altitude here was about 6,500 feet. The smoke-blackened cave had a number of old hearths suggesting regular use by trading parties over a long period of time. I had read Charles Karius and Ivan Champion's account of their epic south to north first crossing of the island, *Across New Guinea from the Fly to the Sepik*, and suspected that the shelter might have been the one used by them in 1927.

At the top of the range we encountered a hut used by hunters, in an area known locally as Mogondabip. Extending through the cloud forest either side of the trail was the fault valley we sought to explore. Using Mogondabip as a springboard, we set off eastwards, investigating caves and sinkholes as we located them.

Although the valley floor ascended gradually, we found our way frequently barred by tottering tower karst, through which we were forever threading our way up, down, over or around. Almost everything was covered in mosses and tangled vegetation. When exposed, the strata revealed a creamy-coloured limestone into which streams gurgled carrying along a mélange of jungle flotsam.

Travel involved teetering about on suspended vegetation and tumbled trees, rarely standing on solid ground. Hidden fissures and shafts were everywhere waiting to ensnare the unwary. Torrential rain was a daily feature and clammy mists permeated everything in the most depressing landscapes either of us had ever encountered.

After five days of this we awoke to our first decent morning. The day started off well enough – perhaps too well in hindsight. There was no rain, and for a change sunbeams penetrated the trees, imparting to everything a pleasant warming glow. I was reminded of my ascent of Mount Hagen with Roy.

Near the bottom of a doline[1] a hint of subterranean blackness caught my eye and I began clearing a route down towards it. I was making good progress when a lofty tree fern blocked my path. I could easily have side-stepped it, but with a freshly honed machete I was feeling devilish, so I took a swipe at the cycad. The blade sliced clean through it, then to my horror the momentum carried it, almost in slow motion, in a wide arc to strike my left knee. For a minute or so I just stood dumbfounded, looking at the blood pumping from my leg. There was no pain. 'Kevan,' I called out. 'I've got a bit of a problem.' He came over and, in a matter of fact tone, said, 'That's going to need a pressure bandage.' There was no suggestion the patrol should be abandoned, so after my leg had been cleaned and bound I volunteered to return to base for treatment, leaving him to continue exploring the valley.

Kevan did a sterling job of dressing the wound. I began a course of tetracycline then cut a stout pole as a makeshift crutch. 'I'll see you in two weeks,' I called out, and limped off down valley.

Progress was slow. For a start the pole was little help, as it repeatedly sank into the forest floor or all but disappeared into the vegetation. After no more than ½ mile, blood began oozing through the dressing and trickling down my shin. I began fretting about the effects of the journey. I had a spare bandage but the Baptist mission was three days away, and involved crossing two mountain ranges. I regarded forests as a metaphor for freedom, and in mind and body I have always aspired to become absorbed into, and at one with my surroundings, to exist wherever possible in harmony rather than conflict with nature. My split second of inattention had put me at variance with the jungle, and now I was suffering for it. Reluctantly I hobbled back to the trail head. Without further ado Kevan decided to abandon the patrol so that we could all of us return together. Yaiyok gallantly offered to carry me all the way on his back. While he was a tireless worker and I was very grateful, I could not allow such a thing. Besides I would never live it down.

I will not dwell on the step-by-step agony of the next two days, except to say it mostly passed in a perspiration-soaked daze. When we reached the Baptist mission at Telefomin, the nurse did an excellent job on my wound, ten stitches in all. But the rigours of the trek back from beyond the mountains had left me feeling weak, and for the time being effectively put me out of action. Kevan meanwhile went on to complete the third and final patrol of the reconnaissance while I remained behind to recover, thanks to the hospitality of Keith Winchcombe, the Assistant District Commissioner.

Audience with a Gourmet

The expedition's departure from England had been delayed by at least two weeks. Kevan instructed our workers to return to the Finim plateau and spend a further eighteen days completing the base, then he himself departing for Goroka to await further news. I remained in Telefomin to recuperate and settled into a life of isolated indolence.

While convalescing I evaluated our achievements. Despite my injury, attacks from the typhus-carrying mite known as the 'bush mokka', a bout of malaria and fungal infections to constantly wet feet – and other places – Kevan and I had every reason to be satisfied. We had in the space of two months cut trails in four separate areas, made contact with local tribesmen, among whom we might at a later date organize labour, and identified over forty speleological objectives.

As mobility gradually returned I began exploring my immediate environs. I met Dan Jorgensson, a Canadian anthropologist studying the Telfol culture. Eventually I moved out of Keith's house and into another dwelling kindly loaned by the administration for eventual occupation by the expedition. Dan was living on a shoestring, and took to the habit of joining me in the evenings.

Dan told me that it was here in the Telefomin area that the last premeditated act of cannibalism had taken place against white people. For years, it seems, the Telfol people had harboured a simmering resentment of the white men's presence and bided their time, awaiting their chance for retribution. On 6 November 1953 they made their move in a coordinated attack that left several people dead.

Two patrol officers, Geoffrey Harris and Gerald Szarka, were patrolling at opposite ends of the Eliptamin valley, to the north of Telefomin, when they were simultaneously ambushed by groups of warriors. Harris died from axe wounds after being surprised in his sleep, while Szarka and constable Buritori were killed in Minimin village. Elsewhere another policeman under Szarka's command was attacked and killed while on a patrol in the same area. Afterwards the bodies were systematically butchered and consumed.

I wanted to learn more about this and asked around, hopeful of finding someone who might shed some first-hand light on the events. One day in one of the satellite villages I made the acquaintance of Kornsep, caretaker of a *haus tamburan*. During conversation I carefully broached the subject of cannibalism. Amazingly he admitted to having been present at the feast following the 1953 massacre.

'Have you eaten human meat?' I asked in Pidgin suspiciously. He was certainly old enough to have taken part.

'*Mi kai-kai em* (Yes I have),' he said with a thin smile.

'*Yu tok stret or mauswara*?'[2] I asked searchingly. He said he was telling the truth and went on to describe the proceedings of the canni-bal meal in such detail that I had little reason to doubt the authenticity of what I was told.

A government patrol post was first established in Telefomin in 1948, four years after RAAF engineers had landed by gliders and constructed an airstrip. Apparently the attack had coincided with widespread opposition to the government presence and a ban on tribal fighting. Moreover, it was believed that failing taro harvests were due directly to the presence of outsiders.

Following the killings the plan had been to capture Telefomin and render the new airstrip unusable, but the Government's rapid response gave them the upper hand and prevented it. Eventually thirty-seven men were rounded up for murder. Of those charged, thirty-two were sentenced to death but had their sentences commuted to jail terms. And so ended one of the most poignant episodes in colonial New Guinea history.

I quizzed Kornsep further. 'Do humans make good eating?' I asked, adding that I thought his ancestors would have liked the taste of 'long pig'. He was now more guarded. I repeated the question. '*Mi no savvi* (I don't know),' came the furtive response. I gave up with this line of questioning, instead asking if I might take a look inside the spirit house.

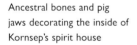

Ancestral bones and pig jaws decorating the inside of Kornsep's spirit house

After half an hour or so of cajoling, Kornsep with some misgiving eventually allowed me inside. It was dim within, but I saw there were no weapons or carvings, but one wall was covered completely with the jawbones of pigs. A large crocodile skull in a corner was accumulating dust, while in an ageing *billum* framed by the jawbones nested a brace of human skulls. I was privileged to have seen these, and I thanked my new friend profusely for allowing me access to the inner sanctum of his spiritual world.

On Thursday 24 July the moment for which I had waited almost two years finally arrived when, watched by myself, Keith Winchcombe, the local *Kiaps* and their wives, a gaggle of excited locals, a police constable, one or two dogs and the odd pig, an ageing Dakota dropped out of the cloud base and levelled off on its final approach. With a puff of dust it touched down then taxied to a halt opposite where I was standing. It was an emotional moment. Few of the team were known to me and this was to be my first opportunity of meeting the explorers with whom I would be working over the coming months.

8 Caverns of the Cassowary Goddess

For generations the island of New Guinea has been a magnet for explorers in pursuit of adventure, from the flamboyant Luigi D'Albertis and debonair Errol Flynn to the enigmatic Ross and the stoical Karius and Champion. It has been so since the first Indonesian slavers made landfall in the eighth century. When the red and white DC3 transport came to a standstill on the apron at Telefomin, the latest thrill-seekers to uphold these pioneering ideals emerged.

First to disembark was a shortish man wearing a tweed jacket and

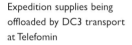

Expedition supplies being offloaded by DC3 transport at Telefomin

dark-rimmed spectacles. Yorkshireman Dave Brook was leader of the venture and a character I had met before back in England. He was a jolly soul with a penchant for puns, well respected, with many important cave discoveries to his credit. Also present were linguist Paul Everett, geologist Steve Crabtree and two biologists, Phil Chapman and Petar Beron, a Bulgarian attached to Sofia University. Once in the field our medical man would be cherub-faced Jon Buchan, while the well-known adventure cameraman Sid Perou would be making a documentary for British television, assisted by soundman Frank Binney of Texas.

The remainder of the team were all speleologists. Mostly postgraduates from Leeds University, their experiences manifold, were gained in such places as Iran, Venezuela, France and Canada. Between them they represented the cream of British cavers and enjoyed a formidable reputation as determined explorers with an impressive string of discoveries to their credit. It was a privilege to be joining such a group.

Over the ensuing week fourteen tonnes of freight arrived by charter when the weather allowed. It was a frenetic time of sorting, checking equipment and organizing supplies into carrier loads for the first month in the field. For me it was time also to catch up on news, greet old friends and forge new friendships. I was especially curious to learn how a large group of disparate personalities, surviving cheek by jowl, would react to the hardships of jungle conditions.

Kevan suggested that the entire team go to the Finim plateau. This would allow newcomers time to acclimatize while simultaneously gaining bushcraft skills. Dividing into smaller groups later, we argued, people could explore more remote areas where conditions were expected to be increasingly demanding. We planned to fly in supplies to Fasanabip, and from there shuttle them by carrier line over the Bahrmans to our advance base.

Being fluent in Pidgin, Kevan was an obvious choice for the van. Mike Farnworth and Jack Sheldon had worked well together during an expedition to Venezuela, so they completed a threesome. Between them they were to apply finishing touches to the bothy, then once radio communication was established the transfer of the whole team could go ahead.

For reasons beyond our control the airlift was cancelled, but fortunately within a few days of the advance party leaving we had established a viable carrier line through to the Finim Tel, and the remainder of the team, myself included, made the three-day inward trek. To the uninitiated the forest trails proved onerous. Tales were legion, some believed, of boa

The Finim Tel advance camp
during the British caving
expedition. Mount Aiyang
can just be glimpsed
through the trees

The Finim Tel advance camp during the British caving expedition. Mount Aiyang can just be glimpsed through the trees

constrictors that could drop unannounced from the trees and crush a person to death – three coils was all it took – so rumour had it.

Despite the attractions of a salubrious camp life, everyone was impatient to begin exploring the caves. The first order of business was to investigate the features found during the reconnaissance, La Buum Tém being top of the agenda. I watched as Pete Gray abseiled the fine shaft. I could hear thrashing as for the first few yards he fought his way through the luxuriant growths clinging to the sides, then, whooping and free-hanging clear of the verdant mantle, he continued. From my perch I saw him slide out of sight down the remaining 200 feet of rope, and heard clattering noises on the boulder floor below. Peering down, a brooklet caught my eye, sparkling as it fell through a sunbeam angling down from the surface.

Unfortunately the shaft was blocked. Attention then switched to the two rock-walled pits due south of camp. Once again these impressive voids ended in impenetrable boulder ruckles, or lathe-thin fissures. Our only surprises here were the discovery of a resident tree kangaroo and an unwelcome preponderance of a potent species of stinging tree.

Over time several minor caves and deep shafts were painstakingly explored and mapped, but significant discoveries proved illusive. None penetrated to the great depth of which we hoped. The days slipped by.

Each night the rains beat a tattoo on the fly and the grooved leaves of *pandans* ran like storm gutters, filling our water butts, and any boots that were inadvertently left out. And with each fruitless sortie into the forest one despondent group after another returned to camp.

Morale was failing fast. People were developing tropical ulcers and other debilitating complaints, while a crop of injuries resulted from inexperienced handling of machetes. Jon Buchan found his mornings punctuated by ever-longer queues for treatment. It was imperative that momentum be maintained, and those who were fit enough continued chopping tracks in search of major caves.

In spite of the disappointments the Finim had its attractions. No part of the day could match the first hour after dawn, when the bush steamed in the rising heat of day. This was the result of an interface mist formed when chill night air, trapped in the basin-like region of the plateau, mingled with warmer air rising and spilling over the Hindenburg Wall from the Papuan lowlands.

One morning, refusing to rise, I lay beneath my mosquito net reading *Savage New Guinea*, oblivious to those around me organizing themselves for time underground. The day before, I had stumbled on a trail and received a bamboo sliver through the middle finger of my right hand. All night my hand had throbbed, and the offending

Expedition bothy on the Finim Tel plateau, in the Hindenburg Mountains

digit was now a glorious technicolour and swollen to the size of a walnut.

Finally I dragged myself upright and sought the expertise of Jon. After treating me, Jon told me with a smile that he was off searching for a sinkhole that had so far proved illusive. Later he returned defeated after fighting the whole day through the forest understorey. He told me how he had been frustrated by a three-dimensional puzzle of deep grykes, dolines and a tumbled landscape.

I had occasion to ask myself what it is that draws people to these torrid zones. Some, like ourselves, came to find something, others to leave something behind. Still more endure the jungle to confront their worst fears, maybe to discover their inner self, perhaps because they are restless and can think of nowhere better to be. Whatever the reasons, after a period in the jungle matters that once seemed important – employment, a secure future, the trappings of city life – suddenly seem of scant consequence. My time here was fast becoming a way of life. I had already been in the field nearly four months and did not relish thoughts of civilization and all that a return entailed. For my fellow explorers six weeks on this plateau had brought little gain. Some were already saying what everyone was secretly thinking: apart from the rock-walled shafts, larger caves existed back in Britain.

Eureka Moment

One day Jon suggested that a group of invalids accompany him for a convalescent stroll. A few days earlier I had had a conversation with one of our newest recruits, a hunter called Numeia. He had whispered about a great cave to the south-west of camp. I was intrigued, and when I mentioned it to the others Jon suggested that Alan Goulbourne and the geologist take a look.

Later, when myself and others returned hot and bothered after yet another fruitless day, we found the camp buzzing with a carnival atmosphere. Jon and his 'patients' recounted how for three hours they had followed their guide along scarcely visible hunting paths, halting only when an enormous bowl, 1,500 feet across and at least 300 feet deep, appeared at their feet. With aches and pains forgotten they had eagerly explored. This was Selminum Tém.

The trio had traced a handsome gallery, astounded, when over the space of ¼ mile it had rapidly increased in size. It was a caver's dream, our 'Eureka moment'. Although eager to continue, there was still the fact of their invalid status, so reluctantly they turned around.

The next day a group, including me, set off. From the eastern rim of the doline we entered an enchanting world of giant arum lilies, ferns and plantains, our footfalls hushed by the generous leaf litter of the sub-forest floor. Eighty feet up a soaring rock face, a large portal gave access to a short section of fossil

Negotiating high-altitude bamboo swamps in the remote Hindenburg Mountains

passageway. This held no interest except two curious man-made pits, of whose origin or purpose our guide claimed no knowledge. Selminum Tém itself was located in the base of the depression.

At the foot of the cliff the vegetation, we noticed, gyrated mysteriously – a phenomenon that had drawn the others to this point. As we parted the undergrowth, a wide opening breathed a cool draught. We ducked inside to find ourselves shambling down a boulder slope in the receding twilight. Just ahead I saw my friends' caplamps. With the roof out of sight and the gunmetal walls drifting apart, we strolled along in awe, leaving Man Friday footprints in the dried silt deposits. At a sweeping, right-hand bend a stream crashed in from our left, but ignoring this we gasped with delight as the passageway ahead expanded into a magnificent tunnel, 150 feet in diameter.

Glancing at the rock architecture, I tried to imagine the volume of water that had once barrelled along these galleries. Lured on by shouts in the distance, I picked my way through a jumble of angular boulders,

© NG75 BRITISH CAVING EXPEDITION

Part of the main trunk route of Selminum Tém

then trekked with a raging thirst over undulating sand dunes. The limestone walls had a pebbled texture, how I imagined the hide of a dinosaur, khaki-brown in colour, streaked with burnt sienna. I passed a group of stalagmites curiously like fried eggs.

It was agreed that we would follow the convention of astronomy and space flight when naming features of the system. Thus over several expeditions we boldly went where no man had been before. Through Warp Drive, the Apennines and the even larger Copernicus Cavern, our shouts echoed by the cathedral-like grandeur, the roof throughout scooped and pierced by solutional hollows and fissures, everywhere striated and rippled by the power of some long-gone river.

Gradually as we explored the length of the system, so our trips grew in duration, until teams were spending as much as fourteen hours underground, surfacing exhausted but elated by further revelations. Tycho, Orion, the rugged Coprates Canyon and the Stargate were added to the cave's features, as well as the decorated Newton Cavern, beyond which the cave became more richly endowed with crystal grottoes, stalactites and other subterranean jewels.

We concluded that a wide ledge outside the upper cave would make an excellent campsite, conveniently protected as it was by an overhang. A dozen or more people arrived, eager for a slice of the action. Mealtimes were suddenly jolly affairs, with little thought given to illness or injury, discussions focusing instead on the latest underground wonders. In a part of the cave named Kepler we had marvelled at the vaulted architecture, and left our silent footprints in the fine dust of Moondust Oxbow.

The Astrodome in Selminum Tém

Like everyone I enjoyed my time lounging around the campfire. It was a time for comparing survey notes, for relaxation and jokes, and equally important in the endless fight to keep feet dry and free from fungal infection. We had lengthy discussions, and talks of a trite nature with our native helpers. Conscious that their world perhaps ended at the next mountain ridge, we tried explaining the great distances to our home countries. Even more difficult to convey was the concept of men walking on the surface of the moon.

Mealtimes were always sociable occasions. They provided an opportunity for culinary experimentation, the principal ingredient being soya meat substitute, though to our lasting delight we also enjoyed choices of dessert, including dried fruit salad with custard. The most popular luxury foods – tinned herrings, cheese and even French paté – were complemented by a welcome variety of spices, pickles and chutneys.

Culinary variation came from

another quarter too. Whenever our camp hands returned from hunting we were invariably offered the choicest morsels. On one occasion I recall a Wokkamin returning with a billy can full of chrysalids, which were boiled up and handed around like sweets. The taste resembled prawns. Perhaps because he was a biologist Phil Chapman made a point about eating the testicles of a *cus-cus* (possum), then afterwards incurred our mirth when for two days he was confined to his bed, retching in agony.

In Selminum Tém exploration continued unabated, its complexity revealing itself in a confusing, three-dimensional labyrinth of well-watered conduits rambling beneath the main trunk route. With a length so far of 9 miles the cave was approaching that of Exit Cave in New Zealand, the current record holder for the southern hemisphere's longest. Everyone sought the extra miles with renewed determination.

We had decided at the outset that one person would remain in Telefomin on a rota basis, manning the base radio and forwarding essential supplies to the field camps. The MAF had agreed that, space permitting, we could have lifts to or from Telefomin. I was due for my turn, so with the Bahrman range behind me I strode into Fasanabip, and caught the first available Cessna to Telefomin. Time at base was always something to look forward to. The emphasis here was on tinned and luxury foodstuffs. Because we had access to a wood burning stove we also baked bread, delicious cakes and puddings. We even had home brew! It was a wonder anyone ever returned to the scrum of life in the field.

At the appointed time each day I manned the transceiver and was treated to news that Selminum Tém continued to expand, every transmission providing fascinating new details to whet the appetite. One team had progressed over a mile down a large gallery, and at what they called the Keyhole saw a soft green flush illuminating boulders tumbling in from a hitherto unsuspected exit.

Elsewhere, Mike Farnworth and our linguist, Paul Everett, together abseiled into an obscure pit, and while surveying the flood-prone streamways 70 feet below entered a connecting passage. Paul had noticed some strange bones protruding from the walls. He carefully removed a rib, and back in camp Jon carried out a 'post-mortem'. The Geological Survey of PNG was subsequently advised that the fossil of a large Miocene marine mammal had been discovered.

A cave explorer abseiling into the huge Selminum doline. He can be seen (dressed in yellow and red) slightly to the right of the picture centre

© NG75 BRITISH CAVING EXPEDITION

The Wrath of Afek

Almost every day we received requests from the Finim camp for more rice, spare boots, etc. There were therefore always carriers going back and forth. Mail from the UK was also eagerly awaited. This we would parcel up and hand the next morning to any porter leaving for the mountains. Amazingly, when all the flights matched, it was possible for those camping on the ledge outside the cave to receive letters from halfway around the world in just seven days.

My week at base was almost over when one day the radio crackled into life:

'Uniform Mike mobile to Telefomin. Do you copy? Over.'

'Uniform Mike mobile. Go ahead. Over.' I responded.

'Crabby's taken a fall, but has been safely evacuated from the cave. He's stable. Jon has everything under control. Over.'

We were horror-struck. Steve, the geologist, was the youngest member of the team and his accident was certain to affect everyone. At this stage those of us in Telefomin were unaware just how serious the fall had been. The news was most worrying. Three days later I departed for the Finim Tel, keen to be back among the action and eager for news of Steve.

When I eventually reached Finim camp I enquired after Steve. It appeared that he had been travelling with Jack through a part of the cave called Tranquillity when he plummeted 20 feet from a boulder. The fall had left him with a suspected skull fracture. His helmet had been crushed in the accident but had clearly saved his life. I was told that an efficient seven-hour stretcher haul had seen him safely removed to the surface.

I immediately set off for the cave. At the entrance I found Jon tending Steve. 'How's he doing?' I asked with concern. He was unconscious, and I could see he was heavily bruised, with a livid wound to his forehead.

Expedition doctor, Jon Buchan, tends to Steve Crabtree after his accident

© NG75 BRITISH CAVING EXPEDITION

'Keeps slipping in and out of consciousness,' Jon said.

'How did it happen?' I asked.

'Not sure, Jack thinks he slipped on gravel, then lost his balance. His backpack then did the rest.'

'Will he be OK here?'

'Unless there's a complication,' Jon said. 'I can treat him just as well here as in a hospital.' As insurance against further deterioration Dave Brook had taken the decision to construct a helipad near the doline. Carpentaria Exploration had already been informed of the accident and put on standby in case Steve's condition worsened. It was a time for soul-searching.

The carriers too were visibly nervous, withdrawn. When asked what was troubling them they told us the spirits were angry; they believed Steve's accident was the result of violating the sanctity of the cave. Moreover, they said the ground upon which they had been instructed to build the helipad was also sacred. With haunted expressions they explained that one of them would be next. They wanted to leave.

When asked about the importance of Selminum Tém the porters were tight-lipped. It was not until two days later, when the keeper of a *haus tamburan* in Wokkamin territory below the Wall came forward, that the cultural significance of the site emerged.

He explained how his tribe shared a common genesis with all the Min-speaking people of the surrounding mountains. Central to this creation myth was Afek, a mother goddess figure who manifested as a cassowary. According to tradition Afek had created features of the landscape, tribes and spirit houses throughout the Fly-Sepik divide. Her handiwork included the Selminum doline and its two caves. The upper one she had designated a place to hunt flying fox, but the lowermost cave was *tambu*, reserved for her own use.

During our remaining months in these mountains the amazing tale of Afek became a constantly recurring theme, used to explain the existence of other caves and major topographical features. The spiritual gravity of the cave became even more intriguing when a photographing party stumbled upon charcoal, burnt *bom-boms* and a crude engraving of a bird about 200 feet into the cave.

At the outset the accident resulted in a loss of momentum, but this soon passed. Many of our carriers came from outside the immediate area, and so exploration resumed without further disruption. Thankfully Steve recovered sufficiently to walk to Fasanabip,

Bush country in the remote
Hindenburg Mountains

from where he was flown to Telefomin. Here he stayed for the remainder of the expedition, acting as radio operator and co-ordinator of supplies.

Through the Stargate

Owing to the accident the group that found the Keyhole exit had left a number of promising unexplored leads. Mike Farnworth, Dick Willis and I now took up the baton. After perspiring for a mile through Newton Cavern, then Orion, we were halted by a vertical drop into a huge trench. Here an easy 25 foot rope descent deposited us in Coprates Canyon.

Turning east we followed the canyon 'upstream', here with a width of 200 feet where past river action had undercut the passage at floor level. We waded through occasional pools to where, at the Stargate, the colossal trench ended and we were presented with a choice of possible routes. We found our way at floor level beneath the west wall of the passage. Getting down on our stomachs we crawled, inch by inch, with helmets scraping the low roof. We came to where the roof had caved in, then cautiously threading our way forward followed an air current through the resulting chaos.

Once beyond this obstacle we were able to progress upright again. Passing a stream inlet we traced the tomb-silent galleries for a further 150 yards before squeezing upwards through a body-sized opening in the floor of a lofty chamber, the Astrodome, which was 50 feet across and high with a circular 'cupola' scooped out of a ceiling decorated with a frieze of stalagtites.

Moving northwards out of the Astrodome, we stopped beneath a lowering roof alongside a pool which received water from a roof fissure. We turned a bend and caught the first glimmering of green light from a boulder slope rising towards the surface. After five hours' continuous progress we had finally reached the Keyhole; the threshold of the great unknown now beckoned.

Climbing to a high ledge along the right-hand wall we came to a window through which we reached the unexplored gallery. We entered a superb tunnel with a boulder slope leading into a chamber containing unusual, free-standing formations. To our right through a low arch we passed along a boulder-strewn passageway hung everywhere with slender white stalactites.

Stretching ahead now was a gallery of a height and width I guessed to be 30 feet or more. The floor was strewn with an assortment of stream-washed cobbles and angular rocks that had us wobbling and struggling to maintain dignified motion. The passage now proceeded due east. It seemed

A chamber in Bem Tem, a fossil cave passage discovered by the British expedition

Highly decorated villager
from the headwaters of the
Sepik River

strange travelling along this timeless adit, abandoned by the stream that aeons ago had flowed noisily this way.

We came across a jungle green streaming down skylights that pierced the knobbly ceiling. Slender vines elsewhere lowered their tendrils searchingly down narrow fissures to form a flimsy link between the two worlds. More calcite formations loomed phantom-like out of the gloom, the whole effect having a Tolkien feel about it. Now and then a cave swiftlet swished by emitting the staccato click-clicking with which they navigate the cave night.

After about ¼ mile of this, the scuffing of our protective helmets on a lowering roof broke the charm, and soon we emerged blinking into a jungle-choked depression. With our senses finely honed by our time underground we rediscovered the full nuance of natural sounds and aromas: the air had a pleasant wet-freshness to it. We saw other holes nearby, mysterious and alluring, diving back into the underworld.

Later, in an effort to link the various Selminum Tém entrances by surface traverse we explored a trio of small caves, some deep shafts and the exciting but frightfully flood-prone Ok Tém river cave. After these finds, however, the Finim rapidly became subject to the law of diminishing returns. Moreover, word was carried to camp that a grand *sing-sing* was arriving in Telefomin to celebrate National Day. With the expedition now at its halfway point this provided a convenient excuse for a return to base.

As I trekked back, I was overtaken by small groups of tribesmen heading for Telefomin. Some were carrying live pigs, trussed up and dangling by their legs from poles. Even so burdened they danced easily across slippery log bridges, shouting happily and kicking their legs high behind them in a demonstration of showmanship.

The Burial Caves of the Tifalmin

As our Telefomin sabbatical came to a close a crisis occurred. Frank Binney dismayed everyone by announcing he was resigning forthwith as assistant cameraman, and would also be leaving the expedition. Even worse, due to an earlier delay in clearing filmstock through customs, Sid now was desperately short of sequences

Ancestral carving in Sepik
River spirit house

featuring the opening stages of the venture. So we returned to the Finim.

A week later, with the action replays safely in the can, Kevan, Pete Gray and I returned over the Bahrmans to the upper Tifalmin valley, intending to spend a few days examining ancestral sites and rock art prior to continuing our journey back to Telefomin in readiness for the move to the fault valley.

While deep shafts and relic caves were known to exist in the wooded heights flanking the Dream River, it was the cult aspect of those nearest habitations that most fascinated Kevan. The staple diet of Tifalmin was dominated by taro, the garden plots scattered everywhere along the lower valley slopes, cultivation even occupying many dolines. Overlooking these allotments, and dotted about the lower foothills and grassy spurs, limestone cliffs stood out like hoary tombstones, while the portals of burial caves watched over villages like long-dimmed eyes.

We began systematically exploring these sites, discussing legends and mythology with the local people. A short distance due south of one hamlet we were shown a smoke-blackened overhanging wall. Beyond the drip line we saw examples of ancestral art, confined mostly to a few diamond motifs executed in red ochre. Even more curious, a number of fissures and solution hollows had been stuffed with human remains, including a well-preserved forearm complete with flesh and fingernails.

Our interest piqued, we entered an arched burial cave ¼ mile further east, known as Bal Kurinan. The dry earthen floor was littered with the remains of many people. I counted at least twenty skulls and associated limbs, but strangely no ribs, a fact which perhaps indicated past cannibal episodes. There were several other rock shelters and cliffs nearby. Each had paintings in some form, more commonly hand prints and lozenges, but also lizard-like zoomorphs.

Curious as these sites were, it was the final location within the inhabited zone where we made our most macabre discovery. Part-way up a sun-baked cliff we entered a short, vertical rift passage known as Wok Dubim Tém. The cave contained the desiccated remains of several individuals stacked one above the other on crude bamboo litters. Each corpse was remarkably preserved, with a face frozen into a grimace reflecting the final embodiment of death. Later we were told that the bodies were the remains of the Winurapmin people killed during conflict over some highly prized pig grease.

As if the finds at Wok Dubim Tém were not enough, before departing for Telefomin we were shown a place where a complete slope had recently been burnt clear of grass by hunters flushing out small mammals. Their actions had revealed a hillside strewn with

The author examining human remains in Bal Kurinan, a burial cave in the upper Tifalmin Valley

Victims of a tribal fight
located in Wok Dubim Tém,
a burial cave in the upper
Tifalmin Valley

human bones, again mostly skulls and limbs. With that we decided that our priorities now rested elsewhere. We offered our farewells to the Tifalmin people and for the very last time turned our backs on the Hindenburg Mountains and the sorcerers' grizzly valley.

9 Into the Den of the Blak Bokis

By the time we arrived back in Telefomin arrangements were already underway to transfer personnel and supplies to the final area of interest, the fault-controlled valley situated high in the Victor Emanuel Mountains to the south of base. To help with this move, a staging camp had been established in the lush Nong valley, roughly at the halfway point. Alan Goulbourne had formed himself into an advance team, and with two local assistants was already there making initial investigations.

Rudimentary bush camp at Mogondabip, Victor Emanuel Mountains

Negotiating bamboo forests in the Fault Valley

Later, during my own time at the Nong camp I spent many exciting days, along with Pete Gray, Kevan Wilde and Alan, exploring and creating a detailed understanding of the ½ mile complex comprising the Nong River Cave. This we suspected was fed by streams sinking at least 3,000 feet higher, perhaps in the fault valley itself, consequently the passages were prone to flooding whenever there was sustained rainfall high in the Victor Emanuels, something it was impossible to predict from our camp.

If the onset of monsoon rains made caving in the Nong frightening, also in the more remote fault valley conditions were appalling. Here morale sank to its lowest ebb, exacerbated by illness, the dreadful karst terrain, technically difficult caves, leeches, dense forest and torrential rains. Days spent in this accursed valley were punctuated by near-fatal skirmishes with underground floods and rockfalls. One entry in my diary read: 'Camp latrines flooded and overflowed yesterday. The communal bed collapsed in the night and we all fell in the shit.'

Descent into a Lost World

Despite the disagreeable conditions, major caves were being discovered, including Terbil Tém, a strenuous pothole that reached the respectable depth of 980 feet. These deep cave systems were painstakingly explored and mapped, despite the hardship. For me, however, the *pièce de résistance* of this final phase of our venture was the prospect of exploring the great undescended shaft Kevan and I had discovered months earlier during the reconnaissance. In the Nong valley we were ideally placed to investigate this promising site.

Four of us therefore set off, and throughout the two-hour hike to the shaft, we were shadowed by a motley crowd of excitable villagers. The night before a man called Tinsook (meaning 'One-Eye') had descended on camp demanding employment. He and his rag-tag band of apparent cut-throats proved to be a hard-working bunch, but they were incapable of undertaking even the most mundane of tasks without a great flourish. If asked to cut a trail through the jungle they would depart with great ceremony, flailing their bush knives, and when they were finished would leave a swathe of destruction wide enough for a London bus.

Whooping and whistling now, and along the way taking perfunctory swipes at the trees with their machetes, Tinsook's entourage had swelled to about thirty men, women and children plus the odd hound and a cloud of over friendly sweat bees.

Along the way to the huge shaft I was racked by second thoughts about the venture. I was not very experienced in using single rope techniques,[1] and the deepest shaft I had ever been down was the 340 foot Gaping Gill, in England, where a year or two earlier a problem with the rope had very nearly killed me. As I recalled from the reconnaissance, the Un Tém Tigiín clearing angled steeply into what was undoubtedly a hole of considerable depth, 300 feet at least by our earlier estimates. But once we arrived at the entrance and I heard the alluring echo of the great unknown, my cold feet vanished.

We enquired of the Faiwolmin hunters if the abyss had any name. 'Tina Bu Tém,' they replied.

'*Callim wanem?*' asked Kevan again.

'Tee-nah-Buu-Tem,' then in Pidgin, with much arm waving, '*Man inap long lukim tasol! I nogat kissim em.*' Roughly this translated as a hole to look at but *not* to go down, and peering over the brink it was easy to understand why. I was told the bottom could not be seen for mist! Moreover, hunters in their pursuit of the *blak bokis*, a popular delicacy in the Highlands, had by all accounts been repulsed in their attempts to climb down using lianas, for the hole, they told us in all sincerity, was bottomless.

From a precarious stance I looked cautiously out into the void. The far wall of the shaft soared another 100 feet or so above, and from every possible niche sprang forth unbridled luxuriance. Each rocky hollow that I saw capable of holding a little humus, every horizontal fissure, ledge or crack, sprouted rampant growths. Swiftlets were whirring about like tiny black boomerangs as a ghostly mist drifted up from below.

When it was announced we were not content simply to look, but intended to descend Tina Bu Tém, the Faiwolmin first regarded us with disbelief but then, warming to our plan, announced that it was fine, adding, '*Yu bai kissim planty blak bokis i kam.*' They wanted us to bring out some flying fox. I checked my shotgun, and packed my rucksack in readiness, tossing in a few cartridges.

Pete was already kitted out in the rope climbing gear needed for the descent, his caving helmet crowning a bearded visage that was beaming from ear to ear. I returned his gaze, wondering what was going through his mind.

'You ready for this?' I asked.

'Aye lad,' came the laconic, but confident, response.

Kevan Wilde descending into a shaft in the Fault Valley

© NG75 BRITISH CAVING EXPEDITION

'Wish I was.' We had 600 feet of line, and this Alan secured to two stout trees. When it became clear that we were serious about going down the hole the Faiwolmin's their expressions of awe turned to distress. One of our Telefomin porters, the fatherly Bimansep, assured them that we were quite capable of descending the hole, rope in one hand while eating *kai-kai* (food) with the other. I sincerely hoped he was right.

By this time Pete had already vanished over the edge. He had not been gone many minutes when he gave a shout that he was clear of the vegetation.

After another fifteen minutes we could hear a distorted rendition of 'Fiddler's Green' drifting up from below as Pete exercised his vocal chords. Then the singing was gradually overwhelmed by a muffled roar. The noise increased until it resembled the sound of a train. We exchanged puzzled glances. The onlookers wailed. Then the source of the noise became clear as a smoke-like out-pouring of flying foxes turned the sky dark.

I was the last to descend. Kevan and Alan had now been swallowed by the void and twenty minutes later a distant echoing – 'ROPE … FREE …' announced that my turn had come. Glancing first at the ludicrously slender rope, my lifeline back into the world I cherished, then at the fractious band of villagers, I could not shake off feelings of vulnerability.

Unable to delay the inevitable any longer I implored my audience that under no circumstances were they to tamper with the rope. '*Yu nogat kissim em na mekim baut na baut samting*. Do you understand?' I said. Thirty grim heads nodded in unison. I threaded the synthetic rope through three bars of my abseiling rack. Shuffling gingerly backwards to the brink, I glanced down, then wished I had not. I stepped into fresh air. I could feel the adrenaline rushing to my legs.

At the outset I had almost to fight my way through the dense vegetation, branches repeatedly snagging at my pack or scraping my face, under a constant barrage of leaves, twigs and stinging forest ants. After about 50 feet I popped free of the tenacious scrub and started to relax a little. A bit further and I chanced a look skywards. The forested mouth of the huge shaft was framing a ragged patch of blue sky. And on this unlikely canvas, a handful of flying fox tumbled and wheeled like beasts from another epoch, daylight shining through translucent wings giving me 'x-ray' pictures of their spindly limbs. With the shaft bathed in daylight my sense of exposure was heightened. The flying foxes were crying like winged banshees, making it difficult to concentrate on the task at hand. I dropped cautiously, like a spider on a very slender thread indeed.

When I reached what I guessed was 300 feet I halted again, to take stock of my surroundings. I had arrived at a ledge scarcely two boots wide. Still safely secured to the rope I looked around. To my amazement I shared the meagre luxury with a number of freshwater crabs, that upon my arrival on the ledge quickly scuttled out of reach of my feet. The bottom was still a long way off. Looking down between my legs I could see my companions moving about like insects in what was clearly a vast cavern.

I resumed the descent, gradually at first, but then more deliberately. Halting once more to peer about me, I observed the slow procession of the walls as I spun on my spider-thread. Small streams, I saw, were emerging from horizontal fissures in the walls and cascading down like delicate lace shawls, the water breaking first into streamers, then a nebulous drifting mist. At last the final few feet of rope slipped through my hands, and I stepped onto a high rubble cone. The shaft proved to be 500 feet deep and was at once the most exciting and the most unnerving I had ever encountered. All around was a confusion of decaying, moss-covered detritus and splintered trees that had fallen foul of gravity.

The subterranean architecture of the shaft merged seamlessly with an immense chamber. On its western side the ceiling was scooped and pitted with hollows and alcoves, and angled downwards to meet the steeply tilted rubble floor. The humid air was thick with ammonia rising from guano beds. We thoroughly examined the chamber, searching for any way at all that might lead to further caverns and greater depth. The floor beneath our feet heaved and pulsed with centipedes, cockroaches and other noisome creatures.

Once it was established that the lowest point of the chamber was impenetrably blocked there was precious little reason to remain. Pete started at once back up the rope. To satisfy the Faiwolmin waiting above, we brought down a few *blak bokis*. Unable to bring myself to kill the creatures, I handed the gun to Kevan. The shot seemed to reverberate endlessly around the chamber, and with an ear-piercing screech countless flying foxes took wing. Suddenly everywhere was a mess of madly gyrating leather wings. So thick was the air with them, that it took merely one shot to bring down a dozen or more. They were hideous to behold, about the size of a rabbit but with a head resembling a German shepherd dog with bulging eyes. They are the largest bats known to mankind and can have a wingspan as great as 5 feet. And what teeth!

Not comfortable with this slaughter, I was eager to be away from the snapping teeth and convulsing wings. I threaded the rope through my jammers, drew in the slack rope and set off for the distant surface. Soon I settled into a routine – legs bend, stand up and reach – progressing up the rope, slowly, rather as an inch worm might.

My breath was laboured, sweat pouring from me as I continued to creep up the rope – legs bend, stand up and reach. There was an unexpected click and my heart missed a beat – it was just a karabiner under tension repositioning itself on my harness. Above me the line felt as taut as a cheese wire, below I could see it snaking down to where Alan and Kevan waited impatiently for their turn. Flying fox continued to wheel around the shaft.

After thirty interminable minutes I found myself once again forcing my way through the tangled mantle at the head of the shaft. Then at length I flopped over the rim and lay for several minutes gasping like a fish out of water.

It was then that matters started going badly wrong. After a further twenty minutes Pete and I were joined on the surface by Kevan. He told us that at a bulge just below the crab ledge he had found the rope badly abraded at a rub point; a rope protector had clearly slipped out of position. Doing the only thing possible, Kevan had pulled up the line and knotted it above the damage, but the rope no longer reached the bottom. Alan was marooned.

Pete gallantly volunteered to abseil back down with another rope and inspect the damage. As he attached the

Remote terrain in the Victor Emanuel range

spare line near the rub point a rock suddenly plummeted from nowhere. We clearly heard Pete's shouted warning. It was not until Alan was safely out that we learned that the rock had struck him a glancing blow.

And so ended an epic descent that had very nearly proved the Faiwolmin correct in their belief that Tina Bu Tém was indeed a hole only to look at.

With the conclusion of our explorations here and in the Fault valley, the expedition was over. Despite the uncomfortable camp conditions and the injuries and problems, we had every reason to feel upbeat. We had explored over 20 miles of new caverns, including the longest in the southern hemisphere. Moreover, the biologists had recorded 400 species of vertebrates new to science, including forty cave-adapted insects.

During my eight months in these remote mountains I had lived through shared hardships and contributed to the discovery and exploration of some of the most amazing caves I had ever seen. The descent into Tina Bu Tém was for me the pinnacle of my achievement, and an appropriate finale to my time in this most fascinating and singular country. For with the expedition at an end I was leaving Papua New Guinea for the present. However, I had a gut feeling that before too long I would be back.

Notes

Chapter 1

1 Until independence in 1975 Australia, in one way or another, administered the affairs of the territories of Papua New Guinea since 1901, when Britain transferred British New Guinea, renaming it Papua, to the new Commonwealth of Australia and, after 1914, when German New Guinea was occupied by Australian forces.

2 Named after Captain Owen Stanley who, in 1849, surveyed the southern coast of New Guinea from the British vessel HMS *Rattlesnake*, from the deck of which he saw these mountains.

3 Several peaks reach 15,000 feet, while around a dozen (in Irian Jaya) top 16,000 feet, some with permanent snow and small glaciers.

4 The Highlands are home to 40 per cent of the country's population.

5 Literally 'one talk' or common language, i.e. someone from the same village or clan. Used as a mode of greeting.

6 Betel nut, the fruit of the species *Areca catechu*, a tall and slender palm originating in India.

7 From Mowgli's song against the people, in *The Second Jungle Book*.

Chapter 2

1 Tree named by Australians for the resemblance of the foliage to the tail plumage of the cassowary bird.

2 The first time white men went into Foré country was in 1934 when two gold prospectors, the Ashton brothers, passed that way. The first government patrol was in 1947.

Chapter 3

1 Gawigl is one of two tongues that are spoken in the Hagen area, the other being Melpa.
2 One of over 300 species of spider indigenous to New Guinea.
3 There are forty-two species of bird of paradise, some thirty-six of them indigenous to the island of New Guinea.
4 Of the family *Paradiseae*.

Chapter 4

1 The Western Highlands province is one of the most populated in the country, with around 350,000 people.

Chapter 5

1 Large parts of the Southern Highlands are inhabited by Huli and Duna tribesmen whose favoured headwear is a wig decorated with everlastings.
2 Derived from the Slovenian *kras*, for a limestone area near Trieste, now universally adopted to describe the world's limestone landscapes.

Chapter 6

1 At least a dozen mountains in Irian Jaya exceed 16,000 feet.
2 A few years later the Civil Aviation Authority decommissioned Keglsugle airstrip for being too dangerous.

Chapter 7

1 A deep depression, often rock-rimmed, formed by the collapse of limestone strata.
2 In Pidgin *mauswara*, literally 'mouth water', means to talk nonsense.

Chapter 9

1 The technique of abseiling down a rope using a mechanical friction device, and ascending again by way of two or three jammers that work through a cam system.

Bibliography

Allen, B., *Into the Crocodile Nest* (Paladin Books, 1989)

Beck, H.M., *Beneath the Cloud Forests* (SpeloProjects, 2003)

Bierre, J., *Savage New Guinea* (Joseph, 1964)

Champion, I.F., *Across New Guinea from the Fly to the Sepik* (Constable, 1932)

D'Albertis, L.M., *New Guinea: What I Did and What I Saw* (2 vols) Sampson Low, London, 1880)

Leahy, M., and Crain, M., *The Land that Time Forgot* (Hurst & Blackett, 1937)

Lindgren, E., *Wildlife in Papua New Guinea* (Golden Press, 1975)

Mackay, R.D., *New Guinea* (Time-Life Books, 1976)

Matthews, R.O., *Tropical Rainforests of the World* (Ted Smart, 1990)

McCarthy, J.K., *Patrol into Yesterday* (Cheshire Publishers, 1963)

Murray, J.H.P., *Recent Explorations in Papua* (Sydney, 1923)

Read, K.E., *The High Valley* (Allen and Unwin, London, 1966)

Reed, S.W., *The Making of Modern New Guinea* (American Philosophical Society, 1943)

Rutgers, A., *Birds of New Guinea* (Methuen, 1970)

Salak, K., *Four Corners: One Woman's Solo Journey into the Heart of Papua New Guinea* (Counterpoint, 2001)

Salisbury, R.F., *From Stone to Steel* (Melbourne University Press, 1962)

Simpson, C., *Plumes and Arrows* (Angus & Robertson, 1962)

Sinclair, J., *The Highlanders* (Jacaranda Press, 1971)

Sinclair, J., *The Wigmen of Papua* (Jacaranda Press, 1973)

Souter, G., *New Guinea: The Last Unknown* (Angus & Robertson, 1963)